WINNER TAKE ALL

WINNER TAKE ALL

*Report of the
Twentieth Century Fund
Task Force on
Reform of the
Presidential Election Process*

*Background Paper by
William R. Keech*

HOLMES & MEIER PUBLISHERS, INC.
New York   London

First published in the United States of America by
Holmes & Meier Publishers, Inc.
30 Irving Place
New York, N.Y. 10003

Published in Great Britain by
Holmes & Meier Publishers, Ltd.
Hillview House
1, Hallswelle Parade, Finchley Road
London NW11 ODL

Library of Congress Cataloging in Publication Data

Twentieth Century Fund. Task Force on Reform of the
    Presidential Election Process.
    Winner take all.

    1. President—United States—Election.   I. Keech,
William R.   II. Title.
KF 4910.T93   324′.21   78-9666
KF4910.T93
ISBN 0-8419-0399-9
ISBN 0-8419-0400-6 pbk.

Manufactured in the United States of America

The Twentieth Century Fund is an independent research foundation which undertakes policy studies of economic, political, and social institutions and issues. The Fund was founded in 1919 and endowed by Edward A. Filene.

Contents

Foreword

The virtues and defects of the Electoral College, one of the most controversial yet durable of our constitutional arrangements, have often been the subject of debate by both scholars and politicians. Heated disputes raged over several elections in the nineteenth century; more recently—in 1960, 1968, and 1976—close contests have generated demands for abolition of the existing system in favor of direct election. Mounting criticism of the presidential election process led the Trustees of the Twentieth Century Fund to approve the establishment of an independent Task Force to examine the Electoral College and the various proposed alternatives to it in the context of the needs of our political system.

Inevitably and properly, the Task Force included both defenders and opponents of the Electoral College. Initially, the opposing sides engaged in spirited debate. The defenders of the Electoral College acknowledged its defects but maintained that the existing system was worth preserving because it embodied certain important values. Their opponents argued that these values, although important, did not compensate for the failure of the current system to guarantee that the candidate with the most popular votes nationwide would in fact be elected to the presidency.

For a long time, the Task Force seemed to agree only on the extent of the disagreement. None of the participants took a constricted or mechanical view of the problem. All recognized that eliminating or even tinkering with the Electoral College might have some critical consequences for the nation's political arrangements. By going over their differences again and again, the members of the Task Force ultimately produced a proposal that artfully solved the problem. In effect, the Task Force agreed to preserve the values that the supporters of the Electoral College sought to preserve, while making virtually certain that the candidate who receives the largest number of popular votes would be elected president, the goal of supporters of direct election.

Every member of the Task Force contributed in one way or another to the recommendations in the report. I must pay special tribute, however, to Jeane Kirkpatrick, who served as chairman for many of the sessions. In addition, the Task Force and the Fund are indebted to William R. Keech, who wrote the factual background paper that accompanies the report of the Task Force, and also served as its rapporteur. Mr. Keech proved an invaluable source of information, as did Judith Best, Lawrence D. Longley, and Richard G. Smolka, all of whom were expert witnesses at various Task Force meetings. In fact, all of those who took part in the deliberations of the Task Force can take pride in having made a fresh contribution to the resolution of what has been an almost perennial conflict. The recommendations of the Task Force should stimulate more enlightened debate and perhaps be accepted as a practical and innovative solution.

M. J. Rossant, DIRECTOR
The Twentieth Century Fund
April 1978

Members of the Task Force

Jeane Kirkpatrick,
co-chairman,
resident scholar,
American Institute for
Public Policy Research,
Washington, D. C.

Stephen Hess,
co-chairman,
senior fellow,
The Brookings Institution,
Washington, D. C.

Patrick Caddell,
polling analyst,
Cambridge Survey Research,
Cambridge, Massachusetts

Thomas Cronin,
professor of political science,
University of Delaware

Heinz Eulau,
William Bennett Munro
Professor of Political Science,
Stanford University

Neal R. Peirce,
journalist,
The National Journal,
Washington, D. C.

Paul Puryear,
vice-chancellor,
University of Massachusetts

Richard Rovere,
political reporter,
The New Yorker,
New York, New York

Arthur M. Schlesinger, Jr.,
Schweitzer Professor
of the Humanities,
The City University of
New York

John Sears,
attorney, Baskin and Sears,
Washington, D. C.

Jill Ruckelshaus,
political activist,
Medina, Washington

Jules Witcover,
political columnist,
The Washington Star,
Washington, D. C.

William R. Keech, rapporteur,
professor of political science,
University of North Carolina
at Chapel Hill

Report of
the Task Force

Almost from the very beginnings of the Republic, the Electoral College has been the subject of controversy. This unique constitutional apparatus established by the founding fathers to elect the President of the United States broke down for the first time in 1800, when the Electoral College failed to award a majority of electoral votes to any candidate. The problem then went to the House of Representatives, which, after six days and thirty-six ballots, finally awarded the election to Thomas Jefferson. In order to prevent that particular impasse from recurring, Congress and the states passed the Twelfth Amendment, which redefined the fundamental rules for the presidential election process, in time for the next election.

In the ensuing one hundred and seventy-five years, the constitutional provisions for the presidential election process have remained unchanged. The Electoral College has weathered great changes—demographic and technological as well as political—in the nature of presidential elections and, more than once in the nation's history, has been challenged. Yet it has endured, in part because it stands for some important and cherished principles, in part because proposals for replacing it have threatened those principles. At the same time, it remains the subject of persistent controversy and criticism, perhaps the most criticized and controversial of all of our constitutional arrangements. The continuing debate, both scholarly and public, over the Electoral College and the many suggestions for either modifying or eliminating its role prompted the establishment of this Task Force, which took on the assignment of arriving at a solution for what has been an intractable problem.

Conflict of Values

Initially, the Task Force saw no way of reconciling what was apparently irreconcilable. Several members of the Task Force were vigorous defenders of the Electoral College, taking the view that the probable consequences, some necessarily unforeseen, of changing the system might amount to a cure that was worse than the disease. Other members were equally vigorous proponents of the merits of direct election—the most widely supported plan for replacing the present system.

3

Faced with these opposing choices, the Task Force appeared to be merely replaying the inconclusive debate that had gone on for so long. Nevertheless, the Task Force's discussions revealed a remarkable degree of consensus on the critical issues of the debate and on the values to be preserved or strengthened in the procedures for electing the president.

So, in spite of the diversity of personal perspectives and individual positions, the Task Force reached agreement on the critical values for the nation's presidential election procedures. It was determined that a fair and democratic system should maximize the likelihood that the candidate with the most popular votes would win, should encourage healthy competition through a strong two-party system (without unduly restricting the development of third parties), should promote greater voter participation, and should sustain the vitality of the federal system.

While these shared values were agreed upon by the Task Force, there were differences of opinion about their relative importance and about the merits of the various plans for maintaining them. Those favoring direct election were primarily interested in seeing that victory went to the candidate with the most popular votes. They feared that, under the existing rules of the Electoral College, the popular vote winner might lose the presidency and that, as a result, the legitimacy of the president chosen by electoral votes would be jeopardized. The defenders of the Electoral College believed that the winner of the popular vote would seldom be denied victory by the Electoral College; that even if he were, the legitimacy of the victor would not be jeopardized; and that, in that event, the threat to legitimacy would be less grave than the threat that a shift to direct elections might pose for the two-party system and federalism.

As it became clear that neither the existing system nor the alternative of direct election resolved the conflict over shared but competing values, the Task Force decided that it could still make a useful contribution to the public debate by clearly stating its differences. It had begun such a review when a new proposal, calling for a genuinely innovative approach, was suggested. Surprisingly, it appeared to satisfy the major concerns of the opposing sides. The proposal was then examined for potential weaknesses. When, in this further scrutiny, it met the tests posed by supporters of both the Electoral College and direct election, it was enthusiastically endorsed by the Task Force as a novel, practical, and constitutional solution.

The National Bonus

Under the existing system, each state has the same number of electoral votes as it has representatives and senators in the Congress. The candidate with the most popular votes in each state is awarded all of the electoral votes from that state. When this existing federal bonus in the interest of the states is tallied in the Electoral College, the prospect arises that the candidate with the most popular votes in the nation may not be the candidate with the most electoral votes.

The main proposal of the Task Force, which it designates as the "national bonus" plan, calls for adding a national pool of electoral votes to the existing state pool of electoral votes. This national pool would consist of two electoral votes for each state (plus the District of Columbia), which would be awarded on a winner-take-all basis to the candidate with the most popular votes nationwide. The state and national pools of electoral votes would then be added together, and the candidate with the majority of electoral votes would be elected to the presidency. Thus, the national bonus virtually eliminates the possibility of defeat for the winner of the most popular votes, which was the priority of proponents of direct election, while preserving those aspects of the existing system that were seen by its defenders as bulwarks of the two-party system and of federalism.

The national bonus would add 102 votes to the present 538, for a total of 640. As a consequence, the existing federal bonus given the states would be balanced by the proposed national bonus given to the winner of the most popular votes nationwide. The Task Force proposal would maintain the desirable features of the existing system *and* virtually assure that the winner of the popular vote in the nation will be the electoral vote winner.

The Task Force recommends certain other changes for the sake of symmetry and simplicity. Under the national bonus plan, there is no need for the office of elector or for the Electoral College. Instead, we recommend that they be abolished so that all electoral votes—those now assigned and those proposed under the national bonus—are allocated automatically on a winner-take-all basis to the popular vote winner in each state and in the nation as a whole. This step would eliminate the possibility of "faithless electors," who vote contrary to the majority of their constituents, an anachronistic fault in the current system.

In the unlikely event that no candidate receives a majority of the total electoral vote count under the national bonus plan, the Task Force recommends that a run-off be held between the two candidates receiving the most popular votes. This contest should take place within thirty days of the first national election, and the candidate who wins a majority of electoral votes would be elected president.

The national bonus plan and the associated recommendations proposed by the Task Force call for a constitutional amendment. If, as we are convinced, our recommendations effectively deal with the problems, present and prospective, that are now widely perceived as flaws in the system, then we are confident that Congress and the public at large will accept the need for a new amendment.

In addition, the Task Force recommends a series of measures to ensure the accuracy, integrity, and speed of the vote count in the states. Specifically, we recommend the extension of automatic vote counting procedures to that small portion of the nation's precincts where they are not now in use. We also recommend a mandatory re-tally of the votes for presidential candidates by an independent authority within a few days of the initial count and transmittal of official statewide vote totals to a national official of constitutional stature, such as the Secretary of State, for certification and publication. In our view, these procedures should be adopted whether or not the existing electoral system is modified.

Advantages of Compromise

Plainly, the national bonus plan proposed by the Task Force represents a compromise. Conceivably, some avowed advocates of either the existing system or direct election will find it a second-best option. Yet because it reduces most of the conflict over values, it is more than that. The Task Force is convinced that the national bonus plan has distinct and significant advantages compared to both the existing Electoral College system and direct election. As against the existing system, it would:

- Virtually assure that the candidate with the most popular votes wins.

- Reduce the possibility of a deadlock and make the contingency election procedure more representative.

- Eliminate the so-called faithless elector.

- Enhance voter equality.

- Encourage greater voter participation.

As against direct election, it would:

- Avoid a proliferation of candidates and help maintain the two-party system.

- Preserve the federal system in the presidential election process.

Mirroring the Popular Vote

No feature of the system is more troublesome—and more vulnerable to criticism—than the possibility that the presidential candidate who comes in second in the national popular vote count can capture the nation's highest office. This possibility is not merely hypothetical. The runners-up in the national count have twice been elected to the presidency—Rutherford B. Hayes in 1876 and Benjamin Harrison in 1888.

Moreover, there have been a number of close calls. For example, there is no way of knowing whether, in 1960, John F. Kennedy or Richard M. Nixon received the most popular votes because of the ambiguity in the ballot count in Alabama. In 1976, a shift of about eight thousand votes in Ohio and Hawaii would have given an electoral victory to Gerald Ford even though he trailed Jimmy Carter by almost 2 million popular votes in the nationwide tally.

The Task Force unanimously believes that awarding the presidency to the runner-up in the popular vote would be undesirable because it would weaken the legitimacy of the presidential office. The national bonus, by providing an extra 102 votes to the popular vote winner, is designed to restrict to an absolute minimum the prospect of an electoral victory by a runner-up. If such a bonus had been in effect in past contests, the winner of the popular vote would have won the most electoral votes in every case.[1]

In the Hayes-Tilden election of 1876, Hayes won by only a single electoral vote. The national bonus would easily have brought the electoral vote result into line with the popular vote total, which gave Tilden a majority. In the Harrison-Cleveland election of 1888, Harrison lost the popular vote but had an electoral vote margin of sixty-five. Since the United States consisted of thirty-eight states at that time (and, since the Twenty-third Amendment had not been added, the District of Columbia would not have been included), under the national bonus Grover Cleveland would have received an additional seventy-six votes, which would have given him an electoral vote victory and made him president.

Because the national popular vote count in 1960 cannot be established precisely, Kennedy, who had an electoral vote majority of eighty-four, would have scored an even bigger victory under the bonus plan, provided he had in fact registered the most popular votes. But *if* Nixon had had a clear majority of the popular vote, the bonus would have given him the presidency.

In 1976, under the national bonus plan, Carter's electoral victory over Ford would have been an even more comfortable one, mirroring his popular vote majority. However, a shift at the polls sufficient to have given Ford a popular vote margin over Carter also would have assured Ford an electoral vote majority under this plan.

Thus, the Task Force recommends the national bonus plan in order to assure the election of the presidential candidate with the greatest number of popular votes.

Dealing with Deadlock

In any election procedure that requires a minimum percentage of votes for victory, provisions must be made for situations in which no candidate reaches the stipulated minimum. The existing system demands an absolute majority of electoral votes; therefore, it has established rules for handling elections in which no one receives a majority. Those rules specify that such an election will be decided in the House of Representatives, where each state will cast a single vote for one of the top three candidates. Most proposals for direct election require that a candidate receive 40 percent of the popular votes for victory and require a run-off election between the top two candidates if no one receives 40 percent.

The members of the Task Force think that the national bonus does more to minimize the need for contingency procedures than almost any other plan that includes a minimum percentage requirement for victory. (Proposals that do not include such a requirement run the risk of producing a winner with very narrow popular support in a fragmented election.) Because even the national bonus does not rule out the mathematical possibility that no candidate would win a majority, rules must be set up to deal with that extremely remote eventuality.

The current contingency procedures are among the most unsatisfactory features of the existing system. Leaving the choice of the president to the House of Representatives seems to many observers to be a violation of the concept of separation of powers. And giving each state only a single vote regardless of population seems to be a violation of democratic principles; more objectionable still is the provision that causes a state with an evenly split delegation to lose even that single vote.

If the contingency election were held in the House and each member had one vote, vote distribution would fall into line with population distribution, as—to a lesser degree—would votes in a contingency election held by a joint session of Congress. But such arrangements still violate the concept of separation of powers. Moreover, given the regularity with which the Democrats have controlled the Congress over the last forty-five years, such arrangements would have a partisan bias.

The Task Force believes that the enactment of the national bonus plan would reduce the need for contingency procedures. In the unlikely event that a contingency election is necessary, we recommend that Congress not be given a direct role. Instead, a run-off election between the two candidates with the highest number of popular votes should be held within thirty days after the first election. Voter support is the main standard of legitimacy in presidential elections, and a run-off has fewer drawbacks than do existing contingency procedures. Thus, as we see it, **the national bonus would reduce the chance of a deadlock and make the contingency procedure for dealing with it fairer and more democratic.**

Eliminating the "Faithless"

An elector is bound primarily by custom, in a few states by pledge or oath and in other states by law, to vote for the presidential candidate of the party that he—or she—represents. Theoretically, an elector can cast his vote for a candidate other than the one in whose name he was chosen an elector.[2] Even though no more than one elector has done this in any single election, the possibility of flouting the popular will should be eliminated. The errant behavior of the faithless elector has not seemed, by itself, to warrant a constitutional amendment. However, the Task Force's recommendation for a constitutional amendment to establish the national bonus plan is accompanied by a recommendation to abolish the office of elector so that all electoral votes will be allocated automatically, on a winner-take-all basis, to the candidate with the largest total of the popular vote in each state and in the nation.

Enhancing Equality

Under the existing system, voters in some states are, to paraphrase George Orwell, more equal than voters in other states. This anomaly is most striking in states with very small populations because they have a fixed number of votes regardless of size, and in very large states, where relatively small numbers of voters can shift large numbers of electoral votes. It has been established that voters in a large state count for more than voters in small states, while medium-sized states in terms of population count for less than either.

Less obvious, and less easy to document, are the advantages accruing to certain groups of voters, such as ethnic minorities, that are disproportionately located in some large states. The fact that certain blocs of voters are more equal than other voters is another serious flaw in the present system.

Here again, the Task Force believes that the national bonus plan, by awarding 102 extra votes to the candidate with the majority of the national popular vote, would reduce imbalances, thereby bringing the election of the president closer to the democratic principle of one man, one vote.

Candidates and Parties

Because the Task Force strongly favors the maintenance of the two-party system, it believes that the presidential election should be the final stage in the selection of the nation's chief executive, and not a preliminary to bargaining among political factions. The Task Force, however, is not necessarily committed to the two major parties. We do not seek to protect them against potential replacements or to discourage the emergence of minor parties as legitimate reflections of ranges of opinion that may not find adequate expression in the major parties. But the Task Force firmly believes that those who lose (or who do not contest) the nomination of their party should be discouraged from entering the general election campaign for the presidency. We believe that candidates who base their campaigns on single issues without prospect for victory or preparation for office-holding should not be encouraged to enter the presidential election process.

Different election systems have a tendency either to facilitate or to deter minor party participation in national elections. The present system actually benefits minor parties with regionally concentrated bases of support while handicapping minor parties whose support is more evenly distributed across the nation. In the 1948 election, for example, the Progressive party and the Dixiecrat party each received almost 2.5 percent of the popular vote. However, the Dixiecrat total came from a small number of states; in contrast, the Progressive total was made up of a small percentage of the vote from many states. Despite an almost equal number of popular votes nationwide, the Dixiecrats registered thirty-nine electoral votes against none for the Progressive party.

The knowledge that only one candidate can win and that ample financing is needed to mount any kind of campaign is a powerful deterrent to minor parties and one-issue candidates. Yet the existing system, with its incentive to regional third parties, could conceivably lead to regional candidates winning enough electoral votes to deny victory to the candidates of the major parties, forcing the election into the House of Representatives. The national bonus plan recommended by the Task Force would minimize this threat by reducing the risk that a third party might deprive the leading candidate of a majority of electoral votes. And the other recommendations proposed by the Task Force would eliminate the possibility of political bargaining with the electors or in the House of Representatives to forestall the election of the winner of the most popular votes.

The alternative of direct election poses an even greater danger to the two-party system. If the rules for direct election simply provide that the candidate with the most votes wins the presidency, without any provision for a run-off, a candidate might emerge as the victor with less than 40 percent of the total vote, resulting in a minority president without enough real support to maintain the legitimacy of the office. A run-off election would solve this problem, but it also would provide an incentive for the initial entry of a number of candidates trying to force a run-off in order to gain bargaining power with the two prospective leading candidates. If the run-off threshold were set high, say at 50 percent, the ultimate winner would undoubtedly enjoy broad support. In a close election, though, a handful of third-party votes might well force a run-off.

At a lower run-off threshold of, say, 40 percent, minor parties and independent candidates would need a total of 20 percent of the vote to force a run-off. Even a 40 percent threshold, however, would be an incentive to minor parties with a national base of support, an incentive that they do not now have in presidential elections.

Although no successful candidate since Abraham Lincoln has received less than 40 percent of the popular vote, a change to direct election might increase the number of parties and candidates competing against the major parties. Because party loyalty among voters has been declining for some years, and the pool of independent voters is increasing, the party system is now especially vulnerable to minor party challenges. Some members of the Task Force also fear that direct election would increase pressure for a national primary, a development that would further accelerate the decline of parties.

Preserving the Federal System

All the members of the Task Force affirm the importance of maintaining the vitality of the federal system. Under direct election, the states would be deprived of their constitutional role in the presidential election process.[3] This might weaken not only state political parties but also the influence of state and local issues in presidential campaigns. Under the national bonus plan, 84 percent of the electoral votes would continue to be allocated on a state-by-state basis, thereby preserving a constitutional role for the states in the election process and a political role for state parties in the conduct of the campaign.

In fact, the Task Force's proposal serves to strengthen the role of the state parties and to promote increased voter interest and participation in one significant respect. Currently, neither major party has a strong incentive to campaign in states that are clearly dominated by the other party because the total electoral votes in the state go to the winner of the state's popular vote whether the margin of victory is large or small. But under the national bonus plan, all votes in all states would be counted in the national popular vote total, which is worth an extra 102 votes. Thus, state parties, even those in states dominated by one party, would have more incentive to campaign aggressively than they do now.

An Honest Count

Despite frequent charges of fraud at the polls, the Task Force, after examining the evidence, is convinced that fraud in the tabulation of votes is not a serious problem in presidential elections. Nor does it believe that the major proposed alternative systems would offer more or less temptation to fraud than the existing system. But there are dangers of human error or computer miscounting that must be minimized if the integrity—and the legitimacy—of the electoral process is to be guaranteed. Accordingly, the Task Force recommends that automatic voting procedures be extended to every precinct in the nation.

The universal use of automatic vote registering and counting procedures will minimize the possibility of fraud or error in any election system. Counting paper ballots leaves room for discretion in tallying ambiguously marked ballots or for mistakes in the tally. The prolonged deadlock over the 1974 contest for the U.S. Senate seat in New Hampshire between John Durkin and Louis Wyman is a graphic example of the problems that can arise when paper ballots are used.

Accordingly, **the Task Force also recommends a mandatory re-tally to assure that official totals are accurate. In addition, we propose that a second, independent authority or agency recheck the tallies of the vote recording devices within a short, specified time after the first tally and that the second total be registered even if the election is neither close nor disputed.** These proposals are specifically designed to lessen the possibility of errors, whether human or mechanical.

Following the certification of the results by the appropriate local and state election officials, the Task Force recommends that they be sent to an appropriate federal constitutional official, such as the Secretary of State, for certification of the official national total.

The Task Force's recommendations for enhancing the integrity of the vote should be implemented under the existing system, under direct election, or under the national bonus plan. An accurate national count, however, would be absolutely essential if direct election were adopted.

A Traditional Reform

After examining the existing system and the various options for reforming or replacing it, the Task Force believes, perhaps immodestly, that its own plan is best. Because the Task Force was divided mainly between defenders of the existing system and supporters of direct election, the first time the national bonus plan was broached, the reaction among some members was that it was an ingenious plan for papering over divisions of opinion. But the subsequent debate over its merits, and a careful comparison of its features to both the existing system and direct election, resulted in broad agreement, by a Task Force that was both diverse and bipartisan, that the national bonus plan was fairer than, and superior to, any other. It introduces novel features to the existing system, but it is a constitutional innovation that is no more novel or ingenious than the original plan for the Electoral College. There can be only one winner in a presidential election, and the proposed provision of a bonus for the candidate with the majority vote is, in our view, in the Anglo-American tradition of winner-take-all. In every sense, it is a reform, not a radical restructuring of the system.

We believe that our recommendations either minimize or eliminate the problems that plague the existing system. We also believe that the national bonus plan avoids potential problems and risks that might be encouraged with direct election. Because it both preserves traditional values and simplifies the presidential election process, it appealed to the Task Force as a whole. It is our hope that it will have a similar appeal to the nation.

Therefore, the Task Force recommends passage of a constitutional amendment with the following central features:

• The President and Vice-President of the United States shall be elected by a majority of electoral votes.

• There shall be a total of 640 electoral votes, consisting of the existing state pool of 538 votes (in which each state is allocated the same number of electoral votes as it has U.S. representatives and senators), and a new national pool of 102 (two for each state plus the District of Columbia). The electoral votes shall be allocated by each state to the candidates for president and vice-president who receive the most popular votes in the state. The national pool shall be automatically allocated to the candidates for president and vice-president who win the most popular votes nationwide.

• In the event that no candidate receives a majority of electoral votes, there shall be a second election between the two candidates with the largest number of votes in the national popular vote. The winner of this run-off election shall be the candidate who receives the majority of electoral votes in the state and national pools.

• Both the office of elector and the Electoral College shall be abolished.

Notes

1. In 1824, John Quincy Adams was chosen as president by Congress when none of the contenders received a majority of the electoral votes, although Andrew Jackson had the most popular votes.

2. The first time an elector voted for someone other than the candidate in whose name he ran was in 1796, when an elector chosen as a Federalist voted for Jefferson. The most recent was when a Washington State Republican voted for Ronald Reagan in 1976. Since the first election, less than a dozen electors have miscast their votes, although six of them have done so since 1948.

3. With direct election, there would be immediate pressures for federal administration of presidential elections, which remains optional under existing procedures and under the changes proposed by the Task Force. Federal policy would have to be established regarding several issues now left to the states, which have been well summarized by Richard G. Smolka in "Possible Consequences of Direct Election of the President," *State Government*, Summer 1977, pp. 134–140:

   (1) How do political parties and candidates obtain a ballot position?

   (2) What uniform type of ballot arrangement—office block, party column, straight ticket option, party position on the ballot—will prevail?

   (3) What will be the uniform qualifications for voting in a national election?

   (4) What rules governing voting—hours, places, method of voting—will apply?

   (5) What will be the standards and procedures for vote-tallying and recounts?

The Task Force believes that insufficient attention has been given these somewhat technical issues by proponents of direct election, and that they would have to be resolved before a direct election system could be implemented. The Task Force's national bonus plan does not rule out a uniform national policy on election administration, but it would be compatible with continued state administration of elections and with continued diversity among the states on these issues.

A Partial Dissent
by Neal R. Peirce

The national bonus plan recommended by the Task Force is an innovative, commendable proposal that might well break the long-standing logjam on electoral college reform. It means that under almost any imaginable circumstances, the presidential candidate with the most votes from the people would be the winner—the overriding priority of any reform. The groups that have long backed direct election should seriously consider shifting to this compromise approach, which seems more likely than direct election to win both congressional approval and the affirmative votes of three-fourths of the states.

I dissent, however, from the Task Force's suggestion that the national bonus plan would be preferable to simple direct election of the president. I do not believe a convincing case has been made that direct election would in any way undermine federalism, the two-party system, or the essential nature of presidential campaigns as they are now conducted. The vitality of federalism rests chiefly on the constitutionally mandated system of congressional representation and the will and capacity of state and local governments to address compelling problems, not on the hocus-pocus of an eighteenth-century vote count system. State parties, the bulwark of the two-party system, would probably be stimulated to greater activity, not discouraged, by a direct vote system because it would eliminate "safe states." Both national and state parties would quickly recognize the need to beat the bushes for votes in every state.

Nor would direct election necessarily motivate many new "fringe" party candidacies, even if the system provided for a run-off election if no candidate received more than 40 percent of the vote. The normal pressures to "vote for a winner" would probably prevail—at least after an election or two—and the fringe parties would quickly learn the futility of their efforts.

Ideally, therefore, I favor a simple direct election amendment; however, as between the existing system, with all its perils, and the national bonus plan, I find the national bonus plan infinitely preferable. Because the effect of the Task Force's recommendation would come so close to direct election, the plan could preclude the need for further amendment of the constitutional provisions for presidential elections for centuries to come.

For contingency elections, however, the Task Force's proposed constitutional amendment should be changed to provide for a direct popular vote run-off. Given the uncertainties that would be created in the nation by a presidential candidate field so fragmented that no candidate received an electoral vote majority in the first election, even with the 102-vote bonus for the popular vote leader, the run-off should be as simple and direct as possible.

The Task Force errs in believing that the procedural questions raised by Richard Smolka and outlined in footnote 3 of the report should logically be any more or less pressing under the bonus plan than under simple direct election. These questions should be addressed even if the existing system is unchanged, since different ballot arrangements and voting rules in various states can affect which candidates win certain blocks of electoral votes—thus affecting the outcome of the entire presidential election. Eugene McCarthy's independent 1976 candidacy is a case in point. Since the lion's share of McCarthy's votes would probably have gone to Carter, McCarthy votes apparently cost Carter four states (Iowa, Maine, Oklahoma, Oregon), or twenty-six electoral votes. If the courts had not eliminated McCarthy's name from the New York ballot, Ford might well have eked out a plurality there—thus winning the electoral college with twelve votes to spare, Carter's national popular vote lead notwithstanding.

Background Paper
by William R. Keech

Acknowledgment

I would like to acknowledge the invaluable
research assistance provided by J. Harry Wray.

I/The Electoral College and Its Alternatives

The Electoral College system, a unique method of choosing a chief executive, was created by the founding fathers for the new Republic not as a direct outgrowth of eighteenth-century political principles but rather as an ad hoc compromise between those who believed in election of the president by Congress and those who believed in popular election. Neal R. Peirce argues in *The People's President* that the Electoral College was not only a compromise but one of the more awkward compromises of the Constitutional Convention. He notes that Carl Becker calls the Electoral College the most unrealistic provision of the Constitution—"the one provision not based solidly on practical experience and precedent"; John Roche called it "merely a jerry-rigged improvisation which has subsequently been endowed with high theoretical content"; and even James Madison explained it in part by citing "a degree of the hurrying influence produced by fatigue and impatience" which one finds in the later stages of such conventions.[1]

But the origins of the Electoral College do not by themselves discredit it. Indeed, many of its features were quickly adapted to changing conditions, such as political parties and widespread suffrage, neither of which was clearly anticipated by the framers. Certain essential features of the Electoral College system, however, remain unchanged. The president is still chosen by a majority of electoral votes, which are apportioned among the states according to the total number of senators and representatives from each state, and if no one candidate has a majority of electoral votes, the election is still decided in the House of Representatives, where each state has a single vote.

The Constitution originally provided that each elector should have two votes, that the person with the largest number of votes over a majority should be president, and that the person with the next largest number of votes should be vice-president. Since the framers of the Constitution did not anticipate the development of political parties, they did not foresee the possibility that a majority of partisan electors might cast both their votes for the same two people, thus giving their party's candidates for president and vice-president the same number of electoral votes. Such was the case in the election of 1800: Thomas Jefferson and Aaron Burr, the Democratic-

Republican candidates for president and vice-president respectively, received the same number of electoral votes. Although Jefferson was eventually declared the winner, a constitutional crisis had come about.

This flaw in the system, made clear in the 1800 election, was corrected by the Twelfth Amendment, which passed in time for the election of 1804. The amendment provided that the electors identify the persons supported for president and vice-president. It further provided that if the election failed to give a candidate a majority of the electoral votes, the House of Representatives would choose from the three candidates with the most electoral votes rather than from the top five.

The Constitution, even as amended, did not instruct the states how to choose electors or how the electors should cast their votes.[2] However, the customs of choosing electors by popular vote and of having electors casting their votes as a bloc for the candidate reaching a plurality were established early in most states.

At most, ten states selected electors in their respective state legislatures for the election of 1800. However, the number declined rapidly during the 1820s in the face of rising democratic sentiment. From 1832 to 1860, South Carolina remained the only state to continue this method of selection. By 1804, popular election of electors had become the most common system, with electors being chosen both in districts within states and by statewide "general ticket" or winner-take-all arrangements. The district system faded, however, because it diluted the strength of prevailing factions in any state compared to other states which cast all of their votes for the statewide victor, and by 1836, every state (with the exception of South Carolina) used the winner-take-all popular vote.[3]

The uniformity of the winner-take-all arrangement remains subject to state discretion, and any state is free to shift to a district or proportional system at any time. In fact, in 1969 Maine adopted a plan whereby two of its electors go to the winner of the statewide popular vote, and the other two go to the winner in each of the state's two congressional districts.[4] Other states have deviated from the winner-take-all pattern on a more ad hoc basis. As will be discussed later, in 1960 Alabama permitted its voters to choose among fifty-five candidates for its eleven electors, and the electors chosen split their votes between Senators Kennedy and Byrd. And, as will also be discussed later, individual "faithless" electors have on occasion voted for someone other than the candidate in whose name they were elected. Deviations from "winner take all" seem to be limited by the desire to maintain and maximize a given state's power in the Electoral College. As long as any state employs the winner-take-all method, incentives are present for the other states to do so as well.

Continuity and Change

Even though many of the grounds for establishing the Electoral College and many features of the system have changed drastically, there may still be good reasons to keep it. But the system is under attack, and its supporters are on the defensive.

It is attacked because it does not count votes equally, and is thus a violation of the one-person one-vote principle that seems to be the most widely accepted standard of political legitimacy in modern America. It is attacked because it can award the presidency to someone who receives fewer votes than someone else and because it can send an unresolved election to the House of Representatives, where, in spite of enormous population differences, each state would have a single vote. It is attacked because it permits electors to violate the preferences of the voters who chose them and because it is said to invite fraud and is vulnerable to deadlock.

These objections derive mainly from a twentieth-century political context in which direct election and majority rule are the democratic norm. In that sense, the objections reflect changes in the political climate. But while other alternatives, such as direct election, more obviously meet the standards of twentieth-century democratic politics, these options are themselves not without serious problems.

Over the years, there have been four leading alternatives to the Electoral College system. Three—the automatic plan, the district plan, and the proportional plan— are basically modifications of the current system; and one—direct election—is a major change. Selection by the legislature, the most common means of selecting chief executives in other western democracies, has never received much support in the United States. The framers of the Constitution thought it violated the carefully engineered separation of powers and left the president a creature of the legislative branch. Selection of the president by the legislature remains an unacceptable alternative because the concepts of separation of powers and of checks and balances have retained their vitality in American politics, and because congressional election of the president would still violate them as well as weaken the presidency.

Direct popular election received some eloquent support at the Constitutional Convention but was rejected in favor of the Electoral College. Now, direct election has become the major alternative to the present system and one with considerable support. When polled, citizens consistently approve of it by large majorities. In the most recent poll, the ratio of support to opposition was 73 percent to 15 percent.[5] Direct election has passed the House of Representatives by a large margin, and only a filibuster has kept it from passing in the Senate.[6]

In the eighteenth century, the ad hoc compromise that resulted in the Electoral College offered considerable advantages over direct election.

1. Direct election would have endangered the delicate compromise between slave states and free states regarding apportionment in the House of Representatives. Under the compromise, representatives and direct taxes were to be apportioned according to the number of free persons in a

state and "three-fifths of all other persons." Thus, slave states would have more weight in the House and in the Electoral College than merited by the number of free persons, but fewer than would be merited by their total populations both slave and free. With direct election, slave states would have a weight equal only to the actual number of persons voting.[7]

2. Direct election demanded uniform standards of suffrage if states that granted the franchise to larger proportions of their population than others were not to gain an unfair advantage. In the early years of the Republic, suffrage was universally limited to white males, but property qualifications differed from state to state. For the popularly elected House of Representatives, letting each state set its own suffrage standards presented no problem, so long as the number of representatives was apportioned fairly among the states. But for a popularly elected president, national standards would have to be established.

3. Direct election would have eliminated the states as independent entities in choosing a president. In 1787, the nation was being formed as a union of several independent sovereignties with jealously guarded identities. The Electoral College allowed them to choose how they would vote and to maximize their weight by bloc voting.

4. Direct election meant accepting the judgment of rank-and-file voters, something eighteenth-century political thinkers were reluctant to do. Property qualifications were designed to limit suffrage to people of wisdom and substance, and the possibility of electors substituting their own judgments for those of their state's voters was not ruled out by the Constitution. Such a practice was not implausible or offensive by the political values of the day.

5. Direct election would have presented voters with difficult choices. The framers did not foresee political parties that would screen candidates and narrow and focus the alternatives. They expected many candidates, and thought that electors would know them better than a mass of voters could.

Each of these five factors strengthened the case for the Electoral College over direct popular vote, but they have all become either irrelevant or at least less relevant than they were.

1. Once the Thirteenth Amendment prohibited involuntary servitude, all former slaves, instead of three-fifths, were counted in apportioning representatives and electors.

2. Once the Fifteenth Amendment was ratified, denial of the vote on grounds of "race, color, or previous condition of servitude" was prohibited.

This amendment was not effectively enforced for almost a century after its passage, which gave southern states the full advantage of the population weight of their former slaves without allowing them political participation. But since the Voting Rights Act of 1965, the Fifteenth Amendment has become a meaningful part of the Constitution. In addition, Amendments XIX, XXIV, and XXVI have prohibited denial of the vote on grounds of sex, "failure to pay any poll tax or other tax," or age for persons eighteen years old or older. Even transients cannot be denied the right to vote for president. Thus, national standards of suffrage now exist, independent of any proposals for change in the system of election.

3. In 1978, although the states remain important governing units, Americans move freely from state to state, and the concept of independent sovereignty has been weakened. Today, national citizenship means far more than state citizenship, and national identity far outweighs state identity. The rationale for states as independent actors in a system of electing a president has therefore also been weakened. But states will continue to be the units according to which senators and representatives are apportioned, as well as vital policymaking units in the federal system.

4. Political scientists continue to debate about the sophistication of the voter,[8] but while some observers find the voter wanting in wisdom, almost no one, including the defenders of the Electoral College, argues that any class of citizens (for example, presidential electors) should be able to interpose their judgments between the voters and the election of a president. (Some analysts of presidential selection processes contend that elites such as party leaders should have disproportionate influence in identifying party nominees for president, but they do not extend the principle to the election itself.) Furthermore, direct election has replaced indirect election in the choice of United States senators (Amendment XVII), and is surely now the most widely accepted standard for selecting high public officials, particularly those who are expected to respond to the interests of large numbers of citizens. Only judges, administrators, and the president are exempt from the principle of direct popular vote.

5. Political parties have existed almost as long as the Constitution, structuring the candidate alternatives and effectively narrowing them, as a rule, to two major options. With the help of the mass media, parties present candidates to the public so that voters do not need to depend on electors in order to know the options.

The Current Alternatives

Although the major objections to direct election have been eliminated and direct election has become the most popular alternative, it still does not have unanimous support. Three proposals for more limited change have enjoyed support from time to time, although none of them has much of a following at present.

The most modest proposed change from the existing system is the automatic plan, which would eliminate electors and automatically translate popular votes into electoral votes exactly as the present system normally does. The change would simply eliminate the possibility that electors chosen because of their allegiance to one candidate might vote for someone else. (For example, in 1976, a Washington Republican elector voted for Ronald Reagan instead of President Ford.)

The district plan, like the automatic plan, would retain electoral votes as the crucial determinant of who wins, and it would retain existing arrangements for the distribution of electoral votes among states, while either eliminating the electors as people or eliminating the possibility that they could vote for anyone other than the candidate in whose name they were elected. The plan would go further, however, eliminating the winner-take-all method of counting a state's vote. The presidential candidate who won the most votes in each congressional district would win that district's electoral vote,[9] and the statewide winner would win the two votes allocated to each state according to its representation in the Senate. Thus, many states would divide their electoral votes among candidates rather than giving them all to the statewide winner. District plan proposals also typically involve a change in the arrangements for contingency election in Congress.

The proportional plan would also continue to allocate electoral votes among the states according to the number of senators and representatives,[10] while eliminating the winner-take-all arrangement. But instead of dividing a state's votes according to which candidate won the state and the congressional districts, it would divide them according to the proportion of the statewide vote each candidate won. Proportional plan proposals typically relax the requirement of a majority of electoral votes in order to avoid frequent contingency elections in the Congress.

Direct popular election is the simplest alternative. It would both eliminate electoral votes and ignore the states or any other subunits of the nation for vote-counting purposes. Popular votes would be added into a single, nationwide total, and the presidency would be awarded to the candidate who won the most votes over a certain threshold, usually 40 percent of the total; a contingency election would be held between the top two candidates if no one reached that percentage. Some proposals demand that the winner receive 50 percent, and a few have set no threshold, awarding the office to the winner of a simple plurality, but the 40 percent cutoff is by far the most common.

Two basic contingency election arrangements are possible when no winner is identified in the main election. A popular run-off election between the top two candidates is almost always connected with the direct popular vote plan, and usually with none of the others, although it is possible to have such a run-off with any of the systems that retain electoral votes.

Most of the proposals that retain electoral votes provide for contingency elections to take place in Congress. The existing procedure, however, has very little support, even among defenders of the Electoral College. The system of having each state cast a single vote in the House of Representatives is the result of an eighteenth-century compromise that is no longer relevant. It diverges sharply from the distribution of population, and it denies a state any vote at all if its delegation is tied.

Almost all proposals to change anything about the existing system include proposals to make the contingency election procedure more representative. Usually, congressional contingency election proposals provide that a joint session of Congress choose from the top two or three candidates with each senator and representative casting one vote, although some plans would make the procedure still more representative of population distributions by leaving the decision to the House alone, with each congressman casting a single vote.

Most of the literature on the Electoral College is designed to make a case for or against it or one of its alternatives. Much of this literature focuses on one aspect of the controversy to the exclusion of other issues that may lead to an alternative conclusion. In contrast, this background paper is not designed to make a case for any presidential election system but rather to present and evaluate the most important arguments regarding the most important issues in the controversy, thereby helping the reader to make an informed judgment. (See Bibliography.)

II/Comparing the Alternatives: The Effect on Voter Equality

All students of the Electoral College recognize that not all votes count equally under that system, but just who benefits from the inequality is much less clear. The sources of the inequality, however, are clear. They are the minimum three electoral votes allocated to every state regardless of size, the winner-take-all distribution of state electoral votes, the assignment of electoral votes to states on the basis of population rather than actual voting turnout, and the assignment of electoral votes to states on the basis of decennial censuses, which recognize population shifts only after they have been in effect for a number of years.[1]

The effects of the three-vote minimum and winner take all on the power of different-sized states and different demographic groups are complex. The assignment of electoral votes on the basis of population rather than turnout clearly protects the power of low turnout states, and enhances the power of the groups within them that do vote. Historically, low turnout enhanced the power of southern whites, who controlled electoral votes which were allocated on the basis of black and white population, but which represented minimal black participation. Since the Voting Rights Act of 1965 and other related changes, black voter participation in the South has increased dramatically. In fact, the South is now the sole regional exception to the general phenomenon of declining participation in national elections. As a result, it is no longer clear who benefits from the assignment of electoral votes by population rather than actual voter participation.

Because electoral votes are reallocated after each decennial census, growing states are penalized in the latter portion of any decade. For example, between 1960 and 1970 the combined populations of Florida, Texas, and California increased by 7,593,000, and as a result of the 1970 census, these states gained a total of nine electoral votes. If 80 percent of that growth had occurred by 1968, these states were underrepresented by about seven votes in the 1968 election.

Small State Advantages in the Electoral College

In at least one respect, the allocation of electoral votes clearly advantages small states. Each state, according to the Constitution, has an electoral vote for each of its congressmen, and a vote for each of its two senators, in spite of enormous variations in state population. This distribution of votes has a distorting effect because each state, regardless of its size, has at least one congressional district. Thus, for example, Alaska's congressman represents the entire population of 304,000, while California's congressional districts have an average of 465,000 inhabitants. When the two votes that represent each state's senators are included, California has one electoral vote for every 445,000 people; Alaska has one for every 101,000.

The Twenty-third Amendment, ratified in 1961, gave the District of Columbia the same number of presidential electors that it would be entitled to if it were a state, "but in no event more than the least populous State." Since the District would be entitled to two members in the House on the basis of population, its voters suffer special discrimination by one-person one-vote standards.

Large State Advantages in the Electoral College

Although the two senatorial electoral votes give small states an advantage over large ones in the number of electoral votes each of their voters can influence, the winner-take-all or "general ticket" system of allocating a state's electoral votes gives large states an advantage. All of a state's votes are awarded to the candidate who receives a plurality of votes. This system erases the votes of those supporting the losers and gives extra weight to the votes of those supporting the winner. As a result, if other voters are evenly divided, each voter in a large state may be able to shift a larger bloc of votes from one candidate to another, even though relative to small state voters they control fewer electoral votes than they would merit on a strictly population basis.

The large and small state advantages come from different kinds of power. The small state advantage, which is derived from a more favorable ratio of voters to electors, is not dependent on the winner-take-all system of counting electoral votes, nor is it affected by the distribution of votes. No matter what the distribution of other votes, small state votes "weigh" slightly more than large state votes.

The large state advantage, which depends on often unstated assumptions about the distribution of votes among candidates in a given state, is more complicated. The advantage is based on a possibility of *shifting* blocs of electoral votes. In principle, a single voter in California could swing forty-five electoral votes, while a single voter in Wyoming could, at most, swing three.

The ability to swing a large bloc of votes, however, is based on the assumption that the large state voters are in fact rather evenly divided, and that competition between the parties is close. If the California votes were skewed in any direction, while the Wyoming votes were evenly divided, the Wyoming voter would become more powerful than the California voter on both grounds: he would have a more favorable ratio of voters to electors *and* a more favorable prospect of shifting electoral votes.[2]

Combining the Large and Small State Advantages

The questions of which advantage outweighs the other and the net distribution of advantages have been the subjects of recent studies. John F. Banzhaf III combined the large and small state advantages into a single index of voting power, which he quantified so that voters in the least powerful state had an index of one, and voters in the most powerful state had some greater index.[3] Using 1960 census data and the 1964 and 1968 distribution of electoral votes, Banzhaf found that the voters with the most power were those in New York (then the state with the most electoral votes). It was more possible for a New Yorker to affect the outcome of an election than for a citizen of Washington, D.C. (by a factor of 3.312 to 1).[4] When John H. Yunker and Lawrence D. Longley applied the Banzhaf index to 1970 census data, they discovered that California, now the largest state, has the most vote power and that Washington, D.C., still has the least.[5]

If the states are grouped by size, the relationship between size and the Banzhaf index of relative voting power is curvilinear; that is, voting power declines as size increases among the smallest states (and within any group of states with the same number of electoral votes). Among states with more than five electoral votes, the index stops declining and begins to rise again. But only the nine largest states have as much voting power as or more than Alaska, the least populous state.[6]

Yunker and Longley used the Banzhaf index to calculate the average power *per citizen-voter* in various states. They found that citizens in Ohio, the sixth largest state, were just above the average, while citizens in Michigan, the seventh largest, were just below. Thus although many small states are advantaged, according to the Banzhaf index, their citizens still have less than the average citizen's voting power, because so many people live in the large, advantaged states. The largest negative deviations from average power per citizen-voter were in Washington, D.C., Oregon, and Nebraska.[7]

In order to draw such conclusions, Banzhaf (along with Yunker and Longley) makes some assumptions that are not fully realistic. He assumes that all voting combinations are equally likely,[8] although he is aware that voters in a solidly one-party state have less chance of changing an outcome by changing their vote than do voters in a similarly sized but more competitive state. Banzhaf does, however, draw a distinction between those inequalities of voting power that are built into the system of counting votes (such as those inherent in the Electoral College) and those that result

Figure 1. Percent Deviations from Average Voting Power under the Present Electoral
College, the Proportional Plan, the District Plan, and the Direct Vote Plan in the 1970s.

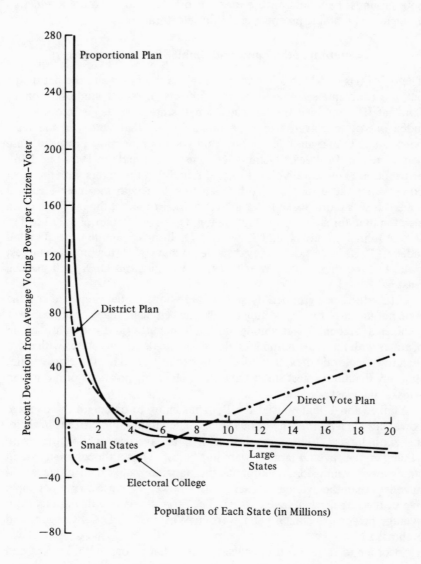

Source: Lawrence D. Longley and Alan G. Braun, *The Politics of Electoral College
Reform* (New Haven: Yale University Press, 1975), p. 120. Reprinted by permission
of Yale University Press. Copyright © 1972 Yale University.

"from the free choice among citizens as to how they use their voting power. . . ."[9]

Banzhaf ignores the competitiveness of a state because it is the result of such free choice, but he acknowledges a distinction between "theoretical voting power," which he measures, and "actual ability to affect the outcome of any particular election,"[10] which he does not. He says that no one can authoritatively say which voting combination will take place most often and, moreover, that such considerations are inappropriate in deliberations about the fairness of voting systems.

Banzhaf may be correct in suggesting that the actual distribution of votes, which changes, should not be used in designing voting systems, which are enduring. However, any description of differences in voting power that does not take the actual distribution of votes into account has a serious shortcoming: unless large states are at least as competitive as small states, estimates based on Banzhaf's analysis will exaggerate large state power.

Seymour Spilerman and David Dickens' analysis of voting power, unlike Banzhaf's, takes the actual competitiveness of the states into account.[11] Using 1960 election data, they measure the effects on outcomes of adding given percentages of votes (4, 8, 12, 16, and 20) to the actual totals for each party.[12] They group these figures into small, medium, and large state categories, and standardize them by comparing the results of a given shift under the Electoral College system with the results that would emerge under direct popular election, that is, with no distortion.

Like Banzhaf, Spilerman and Dickens find that the Electoral College gives large states the greatest advantage, but unlike him, they find it gives the small states the greatest disadvantage. For instance, they find that for large states the Electoral College magnifies a 4 percent shift in popular votes 13.38 times, while for medium-sized states it magnifies the same shift 8.97 times, and for small states 6.95 times.

The differences in findings, while not large, deserve analysis. The Banzhaf study clearly articulates a theoretical explanation for differences in voting power and, by ignoring the actual distribution of votes, has a more general and less timebound relevance. The major drawback of the study is the lack of realism that comes from ignoring actual vote distributions.

In fact, Banzhaf's indices of the ratios between states are based on the joint probability that a voter will cast a decisive vote in his state and that his state will cast a decisive vote in the national election. Since, in any state, the probability of casting a decisive vote is so infinitesimal, figures based on these probabilities may well be distorted.[13]

Spilerman and Dickens' article is more realistic both because it is not based on assumptions that individuals cast decisive votes, and because it takes into account actual distributions of votes. Unfortunately, however, these authors did not attempt to explain the differences between their results and Banzhaf's. Whatever the limitations of Banzhaf's assumptions, his finding that state voting power first drops and then increases with state size is intuitively meaningful because the Electoral College does advantage both the smallest and the largest states, and thus disadvantages middle-sized states.

There is no theoretical reason why Spilerman and Dickens' analysis should not reflect this curvilinear relationship. It probably does not because they aggregate their findings into three size groupings. Since their results for the small and medium states are similar, it could well be that they have averaged and obscured values that would, on a state by state basis, be similar to Banzhaf's.

The inherent drawback in the increased realism in Spilerman and Dickens' article is that their measures are based on figures for a single election; different elections may yield different conclusions, especially if patterns of competition vary.[14] This drawback can be easily overcome by calculating their indices for different elections.

While the two studies differ in their assessment of the effects of the Electoral College system on voting equality, they agree on the effects on voting equality of alternative systems. Both district and proportional plans reverse the large state advantage and place smaller states in a preferred position. In effect, both plans maintain the small state advantage in the allocation of electoral votes, while eliminating the large state advantage by eliminating the statewide winner-take-all feature.

Direct popular vote, of course, eliminates all of these inequalities. By definition, it counts all votes equally: one person, one vote. To many observers, this feature alone makes it superior to the Electoral College. To others, however, voter inequality in the Electoral College compensates for other kinds of inequalities elsewhere in the system. For example, to some it is part of the Great Compromise between large and small states reached at the Constitutional Convention in 1787, in which small states were awarded the same representation in the Senate as large states. Since small states still have an advantage in the Senate, according to this argument, it is appropriate for large states to have an advantage in the Electoral College. Senator John F. Kennedy echoed this view in his defense of the Electoral College:

> It is not only the unit vote for the Presidency we are talking about, but a whole solar system of governmental power. If it is proposed to change the balance of power of one of the elements of the solar system, it is necessary to consider the others.[15]

Therefore, unless there is a simultaneous move to reapportion the United States Senate on a one-person one-vote basis, instituting direct election would indeed eliminate a compensating bias.[16]

The compensation argument is now weaker than it was at the time Senator Kennedy spoke. In 1956, many congressional districts were apportioned in such a way that rural areas were favored over metropolitan areas because state legislatures had not responded to changing population distributions between city and countryside. But in 1964, the Supreme Court ruled that congressional districts had to be roughly equal in size.[17]

Some observers argue that the Court's apportionment decisions should be applied to presidential elections. Since the justices argued that the equal protection clause of the Constitution demands a one-person one-vote standard in legislative elections, in this view, the same should hold for the election of the chief executive. Such a view, of course, ignores the direct constitutional sanction of at least some of the inequalities in the Electoral College. As Alexander Bickel notes:

> The Court has said that the Constitution demands equal apportionment. We should, therefore, reapportion the Presidency. In effect, we must now amend the Constitution to make it mean what the Supreme Court has said it means.[18]

The Advantages of Demographic Groups

In the nation's early years, a citizen of Delaware or Rhode Island may well have held that status to be as important as his status as a citizen of the United States. Different state citizenship may well have meant more than differences in social class, occupational status, urban or rural residence, and so forth. Now, however, state citizenship means far less and is largely a surrogate for other characteristics.

Many defenders of the Electoral College have argued that its voter inequalities make up for other needs or inequalities that, unlike the Senate's, have no constitutional sanction. For example, the Electoral College is said to increase the power of urban ethnic groups and minorities, who are disproportionately concentrated in the large cities of large states. These groups, according to the Electoral College's defenders, are economically deprived, suffer racial discrimination, or have other problems because they live in large cities. As Sayre and Parris put it:

> Yet these metropolitan areas encompass many of the nation's urgent domestic problems—notably hard-core, long-term poverty, with all the social ills it implies, and environmental pollution, which threatens the health of all citizens. . . . Solutions to these problems, moreover, are beyond the capacity of local jurisdictions. . . . The populous states are more nearly microcosms of the future nation than is any other group of states. Moreover, the political persuasions of metropolitan area residents appear to coincide with those of a majority of the nation's voters. . . .[19]

But it is still not clear which demographic groups are advantaged or disadvantaged by the Electoral College, or by any other system. Yunker and Longley have extended Banzhaf's analysis to three types of demographic groups, by multiplying the Banzhaf indices of state vote power by the percentage of a given demographic group in each state. Although sensible and straightforward, this approach still has all the limitations of the Banzhaf study.

They find that, among residential groups, suburban and central city residents are more advantaged, and rural residents are disadvantaged. Residents of the Far West and of the East gain, while residents of the Mountain states and of the South lose. They find that people of foreign stock gain, while blacks suffer.[20]

The disadvantaging of blacks is the only one of Yunker and Longley's findings at serious odds with conventional wisdom.[21] The explanation is that blacks are concentrated not only in major metropolitan areas, which are advantaged, but also in southern states, which are for the most part too small to be advantaged by the winner-take-all system, but too large to be advantaged by the minimum three votes. In the past, residents of these southern states have also been disadvantaged in the Electoral College because the states were not competitive, but such factors are not reflected in Banzhaf's or Yunker and Longley's analyses. (Of course, the biggest *former* electoral disadvantage for most blacks in southern states was that they were not permitted to vote at all.[22])

Spilerman and Dickens' analysis of urban and rural differences yields results that are largely comparable to Yunker and Longley's, and they find that lower income strata are advantaged under most of their hypothetical vote shifts. The main difference between the two studies is that Spilerman and Dickens find nonwhites clearly advantaged relative to non-Catholic whites, and also relative to Catholics for large shifts.[23]

The reasons for this difference are not clear. Because Spilerman and Dickens' study, unlike Yunker and Longley's, takes competition into account, their differences may be the result of the keen competition in 1960 in both southern and urban states, where most blacks were concentrated. Also, Spilerman and Dickens' analysis of racial, religious, and income groups is based on complicated estimates of voting behavior in congressional districts, and these estimates may be highly sensitive to bias.[24] Regrettably, Spilerman and Dickens make no effort to explain the divergence of their findings from those of the previous study. For the time being, the issue is unresolved.

Both studies find that the district and proportional plans, for the most part, have opposite effects on the advantages of various groups from those of the Electoral College. And, of course, direct popular election, by counting all votes equally, eliminates any such demographic effects.

What difference does inequality in voting power make? Banzhaf reflects the conventional wisdom when he argues that candidates will expend higher per capita expenditures of time, money, and promises for groups with higher vote power. He also argues that inequality helps account for the fact that so many presidential candidates have come from large states.[25] Common sense suggests that voters with disproportionate power will receive disproportionate rewards in public policy benefits. The political science literature, however, offers little firm substantiation for these points.[26]

Many observers have concluded that the substantive bias imposed on the presidency by the Electoral College is liberal and internationalist. This may be true, but it is not as apparent as it once was that Congress has an opposite conservative and isolationist bias that needs balancing. A sensible case can be made for balancing the small state biases of the Senate, but it is not clear that the small state bias of the Senate is more divergent from presidential views than is the large state bias of the House.

To some analysts and observers, inequality in voting power, which violates democratic principles that should be an absolute requirement for electing a president,[27] is reason enough to abolish the Electoral College. According to William T. Gossett:

> Clearly, any election system that lessens the power of any individual's vote in order to enlarge another's on whatever grounds, rationale or pretext, is inequitable, unjust and indefensible.[28]

And Neal R. Peirce contends that

> To say that the electoral college should be retained to defend liberalism or big cities leads one down two odious roads; first, a political opportunism in which one would rather have a minority President he agrees with than a popularly chosen one he disagrees with; and secondly, a possibly fatal misreading of the political tea leaves, in which one assumes that the political balances and realities of the past decades will hold true for the 1970's and time to come.[29]

We might expect that those who defend the Electoral College because of the groups it favors would strengthen their arguments by identifying and defending those groups beforehand. This way, if the observer accepted the goals, he could see how close the Electoral College or another system came to meeting them. In fact, most defenses of the Electoral College based on the needs or merits of its beneficiaries do not do this.

Careful analyses should also recognize the tradeoffs. Suppose we were to conclude that blacks deserved extra voting strength and that the Electoral College provides it. Would it still make sense to support the Electoral College for this purpose if at the same time suburbanites, who are presumably much less needy, gained extra voting strength?

Suppose we conclude that blacks deserve extra representation and find that the Electoral College may provide it if the states in which they live are competitive, but not otherwise. Does it make sense to base constitutional principles on such transitory phenomena? Suppose we find that the power of blacks was diluted by their loyalty to one party. Of what value would their advantage in the Electoral College be then?

Given all these difficulties in advantaging groups by the use of electoral districts, it would obviously be much simpler and more efficient just to give any such favored groups multiple votes. As multiple votes were once favored for educated groups because they were presumed to be wiser, a modern egalitarian might favor multiple votes for deprived groups because they are presumed to be needier. We might even seek to distinguish the deserving needy from the slothful and undeserving needy.

There are innumerable inequalities and unfairnesses in politics, and there is no way to eliminate all of them. Even with a one-person one-vote criterion, some people may have disproportionate leisure or energy, which can be used to magnify the effect of their votes. Such differences are inevitable. Congress and the Supreme Court are finding it difficult to eliminate fairly even the inequalities associated with campaign contributions.

But other inequalities are more easily minimized. Those associated with the Electoral College and the district and proportional plans seem not to have a clear, consistent, and convincing rationale. Neither are they inevitable. However, other features of the Electoral College may well make it defensible in spite of its accompanying voter inequalities.

III/Comparing the Alternatives: Does the "Right" Candidate Win?

The Electoral College system of choosing the president does not guarantee the victory of the most preferred candidate. For example, the candidate who wins the most popular votes may not win the most electoral votes. Or alternatively, no candidate may win a majority of electoral votes, sending the election into the House of Representatives, where someone other than the candidate with the most popular support may win. Such possibilities have prompted some of the strongest objections to the present system. Thus, it is important to clarify the relationship between popular votes and election outcomes under both present and alternative voting schemes.

To simplify the analysis in this chapter, we will postpone consideration of the fact that different election systems may lead to different distributions of popular votes. Here we will look at the relationship between existing vote distributions and election outcomes under the Electoral College and alternative voting schemes.

The Runner-Up Victor Issue under the Electoral College

A strong case can be made that the candidates with the most votes did not win the elections of 1824, 1876, 1888, and 1960. Each of these elections reveals the strengths and weaknesses of the Electoral College system—and, at the same time, each also raises questions about the system.

The election of 1824[1] is not very relevant to current issues because only three-quarters of the states actually held popular elections; the remainder chose their electors in state legislatures. Therefore, although Andrew Jackson clearly received a plurality of the votes in the states that did hold popular elections in 1824, it seems inappropriate to assume that the popular vote winner should have won an election that was based only partially on popular votes. Even in the states that held popular elections, Jackson's 41 percent of the votes would not by itself have demonstrated that he was the most preferred candidate because the majority that voted for John Quincy Adams, Henry Clay, or William Crawford might have preferred another of those three to Jackson.

37

The election of 1888[2] is the only undisputed example of a runner-up victory. President Grover Cleveland received 90,000 more votes than Benjamin Harrison out of 11 million cast, but lost decisively in the Electoral College, 233 to 168, because he "wasted" votes with big victories in some states, while only narrowly losing several others. A shift of less than 10,000 votes in his own state of New York could have won the election for Cleveland.

While Cleveland received the most votes, he fell short of a majority, with 48.6 percent. He is considered the candidate most preferred by the voters on the almost always unstated assumption that minor party votes (Prohibition, 2.2 percent and Union Labor, 1.3 percent) would not have gone to Harrison in a two-candidate contest.

Defenders of the Electoral College acknowledge the 1888 deviation but emphasize its remoteness. Almost a century has passed, and it does seem hard to become wrought up over the election·of Benjamin Harrison, whose impact on the nation was not great, or the denial of Grover Cleveland, who after all was elected again in 1892 and got to be president as long as anyone except Franklin Roosevelt.

The 1876 election[3] is not so widely accepted as an example of a runner-up victory because of the apparently widespread corruption and fraud, which were especially concentrated in South Carolina, Florida, and Louisiana. Each of these states sent two different sets of election returns to Washington, one claiming victory for each party. If the Republicans won all three states, their candidate, Rutherford B. Hayes, would win the presidency by a single vote, 185 to 184. Thus, the Democrats needed to win only one of the disputed states, or even a single vote from each of the three. Congress appointed a special commission of eight Republicans and seven Democrats to decide how the electoral votes should be allocated. Not surprisingly, the commission voted eight to seven to accept the Republican figures from all three states.

Under existing law, congressional Democrats might still have blocked the acceptance of the electoral commission's verdict, but instead, a deal was made. The Democrats agreed to accept the Republican victory as certified by the special commission in return for a withdrawal of federal troops from the South, effectively ending Reconstruction. The southerners agreed in return to respect the rights of blacks.

Defenders of the Electoral College are reluctant to accept the 1876 election as an example of the Electoral College awarding the presidency to a candidate who won a minority of the votes. Judith Best, for example, argues that:

> In our centennial year the electoral process was so debased and dishonored by fraud and intimidation that only an eccentric majoritarian would single out the technical runner-up Presidency of Hayes as a matter for criticism and concern.[4]

But in fact, Samuel J. Tilden, the Democratic candidate, won more votes than Hayes, whether Republican or Democratic figures are used. Tilden won more than 50 percent of the vote by either count, and in that sense, 1876 is a clearer example of a runner-up victory than undisputed 1888 because no assumptions need be made about the second choices of minor party supporters.

Best also contends that if not for Democratic intimidation of black voters, Republicans might have won other states as well,[5] and might therefore have had a clear majority of popular votes to go along with their majority of electoral votes. She may well be right, but if so, such a standard would have to be applied to other elections as well. By this standard, the victories of Presidents Cleveland and Wilson would be suspect. By comprehensive criteria of fairness and justice, such a standard is clearly in order, but there is no justification for applying it to 1876 unless we are prepared to apply it to all elections.

If both Republicans and Democrats acknowledged that Tilden won more votes than Hayes, yet Hayes won the presidency through the Electoral College, this election seems to be an acceptable example of a runner-up victory. But the election of 1876 should be even more troublesome to defenders of the Electoral College than is implied simply by the fact that the candidate with the majority of the votes lost the election. The Electoral College defined the context in which the bargain was struck that gave Hayes the presidency in return for the withdrawal of federal troops from the South. As everybody knows, the southerners did not keep their part of the bargain, which provided that they respect and protect the rights of blacks.

As consummated, this bargain had the effect of ending Reconstruction and nullifying most of the gains in human rights won in the post Civil War constitutional amendments. It enabled the South to regain the control of its internal affairs that it had lost on the battlefield, and that it would largely retain until the civil rights victories of the 1960s.

The 1876 election is one of the most consequential in our history. The consequences might have been equally unfortunate if Tilden had won or if Hayes had been able to win without feeling the need to bargain. But the fact remains that the Electoral College defined the rules under which this unsavory bargain was felt to be necessary. This bargain brought about a major setback for the cause of human freedom, equality, and dignity. Surely it must be considered a major failure of the Electoral College, whatever other virtues that system has.

The 1960 election[6] is the least known example of a possible runner-up victory. There is reason to doubt that John F. Kennedy actually won more popular votes than Richard M. Nixon, although it is generally accepted that he did. In a very important sense, the popular vote does not make any difference because it is electoral votes, and not popular votes, that determine the winner of the presidency. However, if it were widely recognized that Kennedy had won fewer popular votes than Nixon, public attitudes toward the 1960 election and the legitimacy of the Electoral College might be different.

The 1960 election has called special attention to the Electoral College for a number of reasons. The reason that has received, by far, the most attention is the alleged fraud in Illinois. Kennedy won very narrowly there, and without Illinois, a few more unpledged electors from other states might have thrown the election into the House. However, even though a certain amount of fraud was acknowledged in Illinois,[7] it was never established that Nixon would have won the state if the count were honest. And Kennedy would have had to lose more electoral votes than those of Illinois to lose the election.

The other reason that the 1960 election raises questions about the Electoral College is the way the election was handled in the state of Alabama, where the names of Kennedy and Nixon were not on the ballot. In Alabama, voters had to choose among electors listed by party, and each voter had eleven votes, one for each elector. There was no doubt that the electors listed under the Republican party would have voted for Richard Nixon, nor that those listed under the Prohibition, National States Rights, and Independent Afro-American Unity parties would have voted for the presidential candidates of their parties: Rutherford Decker, Orval Faubus, and Clennon King, respectively.

The loyalties of the Democratic candidates for elector were not so clear. The candidates, who were listed under the slogan "White Supremacy for the Right," were the victors of an earlier primary and run-off election. Those who won elector slots included five "loyalists" who would vote for their party's national nominee, John Kennedy, and six "unpledged electors," who could be expected to support a states' rights candidate in hopes of throwing the election into the House. Thus, Alabama's voters had no opportunity to award all of their state's electoral votes to the nominee of the Democratic party because, although they had eleven electoral votes, only five candidates for elector would have voted for Kennedy.

All of the Democratic electors won, giving five of Alabama's electoral votes to Kennedy; the other six went to Senator Harry Byrd of Virginia. The problem thus is: With how many popular votes should Kennedy be credited?

The leading Kennedy elector received 318,000 votes, 82,000 more than the highest Nixon elector, and since all Kennedy electors won over all Nixon electors, it seems that Kennedy was preferred to Nixon by Alabama voters. It is on such a margin in Alabama that Kennedy is credited with more votes than Nixon nationwide. On the other hand, the highest unpledged elector received 324,000 votes, almost 6,000 more than the leading Kennedy elector. However, if 324,000 votes are assigned to the national unpledged elector total and Kennedy is assigned the total for his highest elector, then most of the votes of Alabama Democratic electors are counted twice. Most compilations use this system, but doing so clearly distorts the results.

An alternative and seemingly fairer method is to multiply the highest Democratic elector's vote by 5/11 and award that to Kennedy (147,000) because five of the eleven electors were loyalists who voted for him. Similarly, the remaining 6/11 of the highest elector's vote (177,000) would be awarded to the unpledged electors' total vote.

This method avoids double-counting the voters who chose Democratic electors. However, it also gives Kennedy 90,000 fewer voters than Nixon in Alabama (approximately 236,000 to 147,000). Since Kennedy's lead outside Alabama was only 32,000, Nixon would have more popular votes than Kennedy nationwide.

The question is: Who did the voters for Democratic electors in Alabama want for president? On the one hand, Kennedy won every elector he had on the ballot. If an Alabama voter had wanted to cast all his votes for the goals of the unpledged elector movement, he could have voted for all the electors pledged to Orval Faubus, or for all the unpledged electors on the Democratic slate, and five electors on the Faubus slate. But Faubus' slate received only 4,000 votes.

On the other hand, some of those who voted for electors labeled only "Democratic Party" with the rooster symbol and the slogan "White Supremacy for the Right" must have thought that they were voting for the unpledged elector strategy.

There is no way to tell how many votes Kennedy would have received in Alabama in 1960 in a direct election. Since Nixon can be clearly credited with 236,000 votes in Alabama, Kennedy would have needed more than 203,000 votes—over 60 percent of the votes given the highest Alabama Democratic elector—in order to maintain his lead in the nationwide vote totals.[8]

There is no doubt that under the rules of the Electoral College, John Kennedy won the 1960 election. As Best might say, "only an eccentric majoritarian" would care whether Kennedy had more popular votes than Nixon. Because the election came close to being a toss-up, the important thing is that the Electoral College system provided a clear-cut and widely supported set of rules that decisively awarded the presidency to one of the candidates.[9]

Still, the irregularity of these procedures and the denial of a clear choice in Alabama must be considered a drawback of the Electoral College, whatever its other merits. If every state, or even many states, used the legal and constitutional maneuvering possible under the Electoral College system to deny the voters a clear choice, as Alabama did in 1960, the Electoral College could not long maintain its legitimacy.

Of the thirty-seven elections held since 1832 under the Electoral College system, then, three can be said to have produced a runner-up victor. Several more elections came close to producing a victor who ran second in popular votes. Neal R. Peirce lists twenty elections through 1960 in which minor vote shifts could have changed the outcome, although it is not clear how often the requisite vote shifts would have changed the Electoral College outcome without bringing the popular vote total into line with it.[10]

For example, in 1916, Woodrow Wilson would have lost the election if he had had 4,000 fewer votes in California, even though his national plurality was more than half a million. In 1948, Harry Truman could have lost to Dewey in the Electoral College with a shift of less than 30,000 votes in Illinois, California, and Ohio, or the election could have been thrown into the House of Representatives with a shift of 13,000 votes in the latter two states, even though Truman had over 2 million more votes than Dewey.[11]

In the 1968 election, a shift of less than 55,000 votes from Nixon to Humphrey in New Jersey, Missouri, and New Hampshire could have sent the election into the House.[12] In that same election, if Wallace had won North Carolina, South Carolina, and Tennessee instead of running a respectable second, Nixon would have been a single electoral vote or faithless elector away from a contingency election. And, of course, in 1976, a shift of less than 10,000 votes in Ohio and Hawaii could have made Gerald Ford a runner-up victor.

Judith Best raises several sensible caveats about taking the close calls too seriously. She suggests that the very things that might cause strategic shifts in given states would be heard elsewhere, perhaps shifting other votes in such a way as to bring the popular vote into line with the new electoral vote total.[13]

Most defenders of the Electoral College agree that the person with the most votes ought to win but argue that the present system rarely fails to produce that result. Sayre and Parris argue, for example, that only 1888 was a clear-cut case and that "such an occurrence is far less likely today."[14]

Best is more sophisticated than the defenders of the Electoral College who argue simply that the runner-up victor phenomenon is rare, distant, and therefore unlikely. She argues that under some circumstances the runner-up *ought* to win because of the *distribution* of his votes. A runner-up victor "is likely only when a close election coincides with a sectionally imbalanced candidacy or campaign."

> [The Electoral College] discriminates against candidates who rely too heavily on a sectional base. Consequently, it is the electoral-count system that provides the presidential parties with the incentive "to widen and 'flatten out' their vote."
>
> *   *   *
>
> Since the system penalizes candidates who rely on their popular strength in one-party states to give them the popular plurality, the political parties attempt to broaden their candidates' appeal. This unanticipated benefit is ignored by the critics.[15]

This argument suggests that votes in politically homogeneous regions ought to count for less than votes in politically competitive regions, not because different voters are of different worth because of where they live, nor because of how many local sympathizers they have, but rather because of incentive effects. Under the Electoral College, Best suggests, parties have more incentive to seek votes across the country than to pile up a comparable number of votes in a region where they are already strong. In fact, however, under the Electoral College parties have little incentive to seek any votes where they have no hope of a majority. Presumably, a candidate hoping to win more votes than his opponent in a direct election has adequate incentive to broaden his appeal.[16]

Many observers would argue that the candidate with the most votes should be elected regardless of how his votes are distributed. But even if we accept Best's argument that the distribution as well as the number of votes should be weighted in determining victory, the Electoral College encourages broad distribution only on dimensions that are related to geographic differences. Since attitudes on race relations were once distributed by region, the Electoral College helped assure that the Democrats in the era of the Solid South did not gain too much for their special appeals to that region and the peculiar racial institutions that that implied. Thus it was Democrats Tilden and Cleveland who lost the most from the Electoral College.

But why should we assume that the politically relevant dimension on which narrow concentrations of votes are to be discouraged is related to state or region? Suppose Best wanted to encourage candidates to broaden their appeal beyond a single social class? The Electoral College does not help do that at all because social classes and many other divisions are rather evenly distributed across states and regions.

The Runner-Up Victor Issue under Alternative Plans

Since direct popular election awards the presidency to the candidate with the most votes, it would seem by definition to avoid the issue of the runner-up victor. When there are only two candidates, or when one of several wins more than 50 percent of the vote, it does avoid the problem. But if the candidate with the most votes among multiple candidates wins less than 50 percent, he may not be the most preferred candidate because, if given another choice, more than half the people may prefer one of his opponents.

For example, in 1860, Abraham Lincoln received 39.8 percent of the vote; Stephen A. Douglas, 29.4; John C. Breckenridge, 18.2; and John Bell, 12.6. If Douglas was preferred to Lincoln by more than two-thirds of the supporters of Breckenridge and Bell, Douglas would presumably have been the most preferred candidate. Whether the assumptions are correct or not, the example shows that if only first-choice votes are counted and if there is only a single round to the election, minor candidates can draw votes away from a most preferred candidate and deny him the victory he may "deserve."

The most common American method of dealing with this problem is the run-off election between the top two candidates.[17] But there is no guarantee that the most preferred candidate is in the run-off. For example, if there are three candidates with 40, 35, and 25 percent of the vote, respectively, and supporters of the two leading candidates prefer the third candidate to the other one of the leaders, the third candidate could then defeat either of the leaders in a run-off. But he would not make a run-off between the top two. Even though he would be, by most standards, the most preferred candidate, he would be eliminated in the first round.

In a system that normally has two major parties, such a three-way split is not likely, particularly if the major parties maintain their breadth of appeal. In the 1912 election, however, something resembling this problem occurred. In that contest, the nominee of the majority party, incumbent President Taft, ran third, presumably because the Republican vote was split between him and former President Roosevelt, who ran as a Progressive after having been defeated by Taft for the Republican nomination.

Either Taft or Roosevelt might have beaten Wilson in a two-way contest. As the majority party candidate, Taft might well have defeated the candidate of the minority party. As an erstwhile Republican and a Progressive, Roosevelt might well have been able to win normal Republican support against Wilson and also to compete successfully for Wilson's Progressive support.

If we want to be sure that the "right" candidate would have emerged from a run-off between the top two, we must consider whether Roosevelt or Taft was the preferred candidate. The fact that Taft defeated Roosevelt for the nomination does not prove that he was preferred because the convention choice did not directly reflect the preferences of independents and Democrats. In fact, given Roosevelt's defeat of Taft in nine of ten primaries, it is doubtful that even Republican voters preferred Taft over Roosevelt.

If Democratic voters had participated in a two-candidate election between Taft and Roosevelt, the latter would be more likely to win because Taft was a more narrowly partisan figure and because Roosevelt, as noted, would have been better able to appeal to Wilson's Progressive support. But Roosevelt, although perhaps the most preferred candidate among the top three, not only lost the first round, he also came within five percentage points of running third. The possibility that the most preferred candidate may not only lose the first round but also fail to make a run-off is thus a real one.

This example illustrates that even direct election cannot guarantee that the most preferred candidate will win when there are more than two candidates. As long as there are only two candidates, and as long as each vote is meant to count equally regardless of how they are distributed, direct election is clearly superior to the Electoral College or any other system of determining who is the most preferred candidate.

But no election system can guarantee that the most preferred candidate will be chosen when there are more than two candidates.[18] All direct election systems that award the victory to the candidate with the most votes without a run-off or count of second preferences have this limitation; such systems are used in most states for general elections and for primaries as well.

Run-offs reduce but do not eliminate the prospect that the most preferred candidate will lose in a single election. The cost of this benefit is extra effort and expenditure by candidates and their supporters and a possible loss of interest by the voters.

If an election system is to include a run-off provision, one must decide when it should be implemented. Obviously, for the sake of majority rule, one might require a run-off whenever the top candidate won less than 50 percent, as he has in thirteen of the thirty-seven elections since 1832 (not counting 1876), or just over one in three. Five of the cases were in this century, and three since World War II.

For many direct election advocates, that standard would make run-offs too frequent unless there is compelling evidence that the results of a run-off would be different.[19] In order to avoid regular run-offs, most proponents of direct election would award the presidency to the candidate with the most votes over 40 percent, providing for a run-off only if the leading candidate did not reach that level. Only one winning candidate for president has won less than 40 percent of the popular vote. Lincoln won 39.82 percent in 1860, although he might have made 40 percent if he had been allowed on the ballot in the nine southern states that refused him a place.[20] But if there had been a run-off, Lincoln might not have defeated Douglas because many votes that went to Bell and Breckenridge might have gone to Douglas. Although the 40 percent figure is somewhat arbitrary, it minimizes the risk of choosing someone other than the most preferred candidate, and it avoids election of a president with too weak a mandate.

Thus by majoritarian standards, even direct popular vote is somewhat arbitrary when there are more than two candidates. Under those conditions, its superiority to the Electoral College is relative rather than absolute.

Is direct election superior at all when there are more than two candidates? In such a case, the Electoral College exaggerates the strength of plurality winners in each state by awarding them all of the state's electoral votes. Under this system, the plurality winner is most preferred in each state, no matter how low his percentage. Unless the votes of the nationally leading candidate are inefficiently distributed (as Tilden's were in 1876 and Cleveland's were in 1888), the Electoral College then aggregates these electoral votes so that the national plurality winner receives a majority of electoral votes and thus the presidency.

Short of arguments regarding the distribution of votes, such as Best's, the Electoral College system is no less arbitrary than simply awarding the presidency to the candidate with the most votes, and it introduces possibilities of further distortion. If the system is good because it usually awards the victory to the candidate with the most votes, why not simply award it directly to that person? Why should a mere plurality be worth more in a state than it is in the nation?

Among the other alternatives to the Electoral College, the automatic plan would have no effect on outcomes; it would change the votes of only the handful of faithless electors, none of whom decides an election. The district plan, which allows a statewide loser the votes of the congressional districts he wins, could change some outcomes. For example, in the 1972 election, George McGovern won only Massachusetts and the District of Columbia, receiving all seventeen electoral votes those two units had to award. Under the district plan, he would have received forty-seven more electoral votes, adding forty-eight for the number of districts he won in states he lost, and subtracting one for the single Massachusetts district he lost to Nixon.

The district plan retains the winner-take-all feature of the Electoral College but localizes its application to congressional districts, except for the two statewide votes. It still awards an entire electoral vote for a plurality in a district. Unless the distribution of votes among districts in states is highly skewed, the results from the district plan are not likely to be much different than the results from the existing system. For elections between 1952 and 1976 (the only ones for which it has been calculated), Carter and Ford would have tied in 1976 with 269 votes apiece. Nixon would have narrowly won in 1960 with 278 electoral votes.

The proportional plan, by eliminating the winner-take-all feature entirely and therefore no longer exaggerating marginal victories, is a better reflection of the distribution of votes for candidates other than the winner in each state. Thus its results would resemble those of direct popular election, except that it would exaggerate small state voting power by allocating at least three votes to each state. For this reason, the proportional system is much less likely to yield an Electoral College majority than the present system. Accordingly, proportional plans typically award the presidency for some fraction of electoral votes short of a majority, often 40 percent.

When the rules of the proportional plan are applied to elections from 1864 to the present, numerous presidents lose their Electoral College majority. Only five, however, lose their Electoral College plurality. In 1960, Nixon would have led Kennedy by one-half of an electoral vote. In 1896, Bryan would have led McKinley. In 1888, Cleveland would have led Harrison, and in 1880, Hancock would have led Garfield. In 1876, Tilden would have led Hayes.[21] Just who would have won these and other elections under the proportional plan depends on what proportion of the electoral vote was required for victory.

IV/Contingency Election Procedures: A Necessary Evil

Almost every proposed presidential election system sets some minimal level of popular or electoral votes for victory and provides for a second round of some sort in case that level is not reached. The reason for this provision is that no proposed system limits the number of candidates to two, and consequently, each must face the possibility that popular support is so dispersed that no candidate is close to a majority.

Although most states award all offices, from governor and senator on down, to the candidate with the simple plurality, few analysts advocate using such a system to choose the president. The office is considered too important to be awarded to anyone without a strong claim to be the most preferred candidate. A second round presumably substantiates such a claim if the first round does not.

But contingency elections are usually considered necessary evils, and there is a widespread suspicion of any system that seems likely to use them under any but the rarest of conditions. Of course, if a system identifies the most preferred candidate in a single election, the avoidance of a second round is indeed desirable, if only as a saving of time, effort, and money. However, if the first round does not yield a very clear choice, a contingency election that does so may well be worth what it costs.

There is a tradeoff, then, between the goal of avoiding a contingency election and the goal of assuring the choice of the "right" candidate. If the desire to avoid a contingency election is sufficiently strong, the office can simply be awarded to the candidate with the most electoral or popular votes, no matter how small his total. Alternatively, if the desire to assure the victory of the most preferred candidate is sufficiently strong, a run-off can be held whenever no candidate receives a majority of the votes. Any intervening point between these two natural extremes is at least somewhat arbitrary.

Procedures for initial elections and for contingency elections are theoretically independent and can be evaluated separately. That is, either a

47

popular run-off or a congressional contingency election could be joined with either direct election, the present Electoral College system, or any variants.[1] Contingency procedures could be implemented when the top candidate falls below either a majority or some set lower proportion of either electoral votes or popular votes.

One might argue that the level of votes needed to avoid a contingency election should be higher, the more the vote counting system exaggerates the popular vote.

As Table 1 shows, the present Electoral College exaggerates the popular votes the most; it is followed by the district plan; the proportional plan yields results that are very comparable to the actual distribution of votes. (The reason for the small distortion with the proportional plan is the extra weight that it gives to small state voters.)

Table 1
Winner's Percentage of the Votes under Alternative Plans

	1964	1968	1972	1976
Percent of popular vote	61.1	43.4	60.7	50.0
Percent of electoral vote under proportional plan	59.5	43.5	61.4	50.1
Percent of electoral vote under district plan	84.7	53.7	88.1	50.0
Percent of electoral vote under present winner-take-all plan	90.3	56.1	96.8	55.2

Sources: For 1964, Peirce, *The People's President,* pp. 307, 358–359.

For 1968, Polsby and Wildavsky, *Presidential Elections,* fourth edition, p. 253.

For 1972 and 1976, unpublished materials calculated by Joseph B. Gorman of the Congressional Research Service, Congressional Quarterly Publications, and author.

According to this view, it is appropriate for the present winner-take-all system to demand a majority of electoral votes and for the proportional and direct election plans to set lower standards, such as 40 percent. Since the Electoral College normally translates popular vote pluralities of about 40 percent into Electoral College majorities, contingency elections for direct vote plans at 40 percent may be the equivalent of the Electoral College at 50 percent. But, of course, by this rationale, an absolute Electoral College majority may be no less arbitrary than a 40 percent cutoff for direct election. In fact, since the Electoral College can reject a candidate that wins an absolute majority of popular votes, it may be considered more arbitrary.

Contingency Election under the Electoral College

If no candidate wins a majority of electoral votes, the Constitution sends the election to the House of Representatives for a decision by a majority of the votes, with each state casting a single vote. The drafting committee at the Constitutional Convention had originally proposed that the contingency election take place in the Senate, but this proposal was not accepted because it would make the presidency too remote from popular control—the Senate was selected by state legislatures—and because it would further enhance the already substantial powers of the Senate.

Small states opposed giving the House the power to decide contingency elections because they had less strength in the House than they did in the Senate. The provision that each state have a single vote in the House was thus a compromise between those who wanted to make the president a "man of the people" and those in the small states, who did not want their power diluted in the popularly elected House. The issue was carefully considered because many delegates apparently anticipated frequent contingency elections.[2]

Opponents of the Electoral College are especially disturbed by the single vote each state has in contingency elections in the House, and they emphasize the comparisons between California and Alaska, New York and Nevada, and so forth. Moreover, since the ratio of House seats between the largest and smallest states (an indirect measure of population differences) has increased from ten to one to a current forty-three to one, this inequity has become considerably greater than it was originally.

The Electoral College's contingency election procedures have been used only twice,[3] both times in the early nineteenth century. The conditions that necessitated their use are not likely to recur, but as they are the only experience with the system to date, they are worth examining.

The Twelfth Amendment, which provides for separate ballots for president and vice-president, has eliminated the possibility of the situation that forced a contingency election in 1800.[4] In that election, all the electors favorable to a given party cast their votes for the same two candidates, thus producing a tie between the candidates for vice-president and president, leaving the House to resolve the tie. Even the nature of the division in the House is no longer relevant, since it involved Federalists supporting Democratic-Republican vice-presidential candidate Aaron Burr in order to block the election of Democratic-Republican presidential candidate Thomas Jefferson, who was considered by some Federalists to be a dangerous radical. The fact that the contingency election resulted in deadlock is, however, relevant. The initial vote among the sixteen states was eight for Jefferson, six for Burr, and two states not counted because their congressmen were tied. It took thirty-six ballots and six days before Jefferson was named president.[5]

Since the adoption of the Twelfth Amendment contingency election procedures for choosing the president have been needed only once, in 1824,[6] and changes since then in the preliminary procedures have made contingency elections less likely. Since 1832, the winner-take-all system of awarding state electoral votes has been virtually universal, and, since then, the national party conventions have become the accepted mechanism for nominating candidates of the major parties. The former feature exaggerates pluralities into majorities of electoral votes, and the latter helps insure that the parties are able to control access to the ballot. Without these features, state votes might be divided in such a way that the winner's plurality is not magnified into an electoral majority, and dissident candidates for nomination might secure a place on the general election ballot.

In 1824, four men won electoral votes. Andrew Jackson and John Quincy Adams ranked first and second in both popular votes and electoral votes. While Henry Clay ranked third in popular votes, he trailed William H. Crawford in electoral votes, and since the House chooses from the top three, Clay was eliminated. Although Adams had won a majority of electoral votes in only seven states to Jackson's eleven (with thirteen needed to win), the preferences of House delegations were not the same as those of the electors. With Clay's help, Adams added the three states that had gone to Clay, plus Maryland, Louisiana, and Illinois, each of which had cast a majority of its electoral votes for Jackson. Jackson and his followers made much of the fact that he had been denied the presidency in spite of having won the most popular votes; indeed, the 1824 election results were a continuing liability to Adams as president and a major asset to Jackson's 1828 campaign.

Actually, Jackson's claim that he was the choice of the people is weak, even if we assume that he could have won a run-off with any of his competitors. First, his vote totals were based on only eighteen of twenty-four states, because the other six, including New York, the most populous state of all, chose their electors in the legislature without a popular vote. Furthermore, Jackson's claim to popular support was weak in the three states that he won in the Electoral College but lost in the House. In Illinois and Maryland, he had fewer popular votes than Adams but won a majority of the electoral votes because they were awarded on a district system. In Louisiana, the locale of his military triumph, Jackson won a majority of electoral votes in the state legislature, but was denied the state's vote in the popularly elected House. The people of Louisiana had no opportunity to express their preferences among Jackson and his opponents. Jackson's case does have some validity; he did run ahead of Adams in the three states that Clay won and shifted to Adams. Also, Adams never fully escaped the suspicion that he had made a deal to appoint Clay secretary of state in return for his support in the House.[7]

Whatever the subtleties involved in Jackson's loss, he has ever since been seen by many as a popular choice denied the nation's highest office by a procedure of questionable legitimacy. No president would want to be chosen as Adams was if he could possibly help it. Though distant, the 1824 election is not an encouraging precedent.

Even defenders of the Electoral College have little good to say about its contingency election procedure; in fact, they are much less inclined to defend the procedure than they are to argue that it probably will not be needed. Sayre and Parris group it among "other potential calamities . . . that should be dismissed as highly unlikely or virtually irrelevant," and devote less than a page to it.[8] Best takes the issue more seriously and devotes a whole chapter to it under the Electoral College and alternative systems. She acknowledges that the present contingency procedure has defects, such as the "injustices" of only one vote per state regardless of size and no vote at all if the state delegation is tied, and the possibility that the House might select a president and vice-president of different parties.

Assessing the Alternatives

Best analyzes in depth the suggestion that the contingency election be decided in a joint session of Congress with each of the 535 members casting one vote. She ultimately rejects this proposal because she finds its major assumption unwarranted "that a President chosen by a joint session would be more representative of the popular will than one chosen by the House voting by states. . . . It is not at all clear that the suggested system would be a substantive improvement."[9]

She finds the main drawbacks in the joint session proposal to be the fact that "the candidate who did not win the plurality" can be selected, especially if he belonged to the majority party, and that "if there was not a straight partisan vote, backroom deals would blossom in Congress. . . . [This] would place tremendous burdens on Congress that in such a partisan body could prove to be severely dysfunctional."[10]

As discussed earlier, the candidate with the plurality is not necessarily the most preferred candidate, but as Best observes, any contingency election in Congress would stack the deck strongly against the candidate of the congressional minority. Since the Democrats have lost control of Congress only twice since 1932 and not at all since 1954, this is hardly a random bias. It would work strongly against Republicans in this political era.

Best is also correct in suggesting that not all members of Congress would necessarily vote for the candidate of their party, and that the bargaining associated with such deviations "would result in bitterness and suspicions of corrupt deals that would damage the Congress as well as the Presidency."[11] The inference that John Quincy Adams gave Henry Clay the position of secretary of state in return for his support in the 1824 contingency election is a good example of what might occur.

Best argues that "[i]n fact, neither the existing contingency procedure nor the joint-session plan is completely satisfactory." She defends the prevailing arrangements only on the ground that the contingency is so remote. She argues that run-off elections are more desirable if contingency elections are likely to be often necessary.[12]

> In evaluating any contingency-election procedure, the first question should be, How often would a contingency election be necessary? The probability of a contingency election has a direct bearing on its most desirable form, for if the results of a general election are frequently inconclusive, we must seriously consider bringing the people into the contingency process. If the general election does not produce a winner much of the time, a contingency election that is removed from the people will not satisfy democratic criteria. If, however, the general election rarely fails to select a President or does so only under unusual circumstances, we must consider the most prudent and expeditious method of resolving a deadlock.[13]

Best is surely correct in asserting that a victor of a popularly based run-off would have more legitimacy and a stronger claim to the presidency than the victor of a congressional contingency election of any variety. But if such a procedure is more satisfactory for regular procedures, why should it be less so for remote contingencies? Why is an unsatisfactory procedure more "prudent and expeditious" if rarely used than if regularly used? Unless one finds a convincing answer to these questions, it seems that Best's arguments are meritorious, but that they add up to a case for a popular run-off rather than for retaining contingency election in Congress.

If no compelling case can be made for the inherent desirability of the Electoral College's contingency election procedures, the argument that they will not be necessary becomes all the more critical. Best is correct in arguing that both the winner-take-all system of allocating state electoral votes and the national convention system of nominating candidates reduce the likelihood that an election will be thrown into the House. But, as indicated earlier in this chapter, there have been some close calls, the most recent of which was 1968.[14]

Best outlines carefully the conditions under which a minor party candidate might force an election into the House:

> First he must have a strong regional base where he can win electoral votes. Then he must wage a national campaign for popular votes that produces a fairly even electoral vote division between the two major candidates in order to prevent the stronger candidate from getting an electoral majority. If the major parties are evenly matched in potential electoral votes, he must draw equally on the strength of both. If they are not, he must draw more from the stronger.

She likens the situation of the third-party candidate to that of "a parachutist attempting to land on a marker with the winds strong and variable" but notes that "we may take comfort in the fact that [the Wallace phenomenon] illustrated anew the impracticality of a third-party strategy whose object is to deadlock an election."[15]

James A. Michener takes no such comfort. His book, *Presidential Lottery*,[16] revolves around a series of scenarios of deadlock he had anticipated during the 1968 election. While Michener's book is less carefully argued than Best's, and has a breathless, exaggerated quality ("One man—a small, clever, intelligent rabble-rousing judge from Alabama—could determine the destiny of this nation"[17]), Michener does suggest that we came closer to contingency election in 1968 than Best is willing to admit, and his scenarios are not totally implausible.[18] Indeed, Best's own analysis of the conditions for a deadlock strategy (noted above) are a remarkably precise description of the Wallace candidacy.

Longley and Braun have outlined the possible results of the failure of the 1968 election to produce an Electoral College majority. The two major parties might have agreed to join together in support of the candidate who received the Electoral College plurality. Or Wallace might have shifted his electoral votes to one of the major party candidates with or without a "deal." Or, if the election had gone to the House, Humphrey might have won if all votes were by party lines. But if numerous southern congressmen carried out their pledge to vote as their districts had voted, no candidate would have had a majority of states.[19]

None of these alternatives seems clearly preferable to a run-off election. While no disaster occurred, the risks seem to have been great enough to merit serious consideration of the run-off. Why is the run-off considered so undesirable? Best cites the expense, voter fatigue, and a dropoff in participation. She also suggests that the uncertainty "fosters political intrigue and increases the likelihood of violence." A run-off would "shorten the time available for an orderly transition of power," might necessitate a national recount, and would "weaken or alter" the two-party system.[20] Sayre and Parris emphasize that a run-off would encourage minor parties to enter presidential campaigns, and pave the way for them to bargain with the leading contestants in the run-off campaign. They suggest that bargaining in such a context would be less desirable than that which currently takes place before and during the national party conventions because it would be less open and publicized.[21]

Actually, there is no reason to expect that bargaining between direct election and a run-off would be less desirable than that under current contingency procedures. Bargaining is unsavory if it involves secret deals and private gains. For example, if Henry Clay had been appointed secretary of state in 1825 because he had shifted his support to John Quincy Adams in the House contingency election, he could be considered to have struck an unsavory bargain for private gain. If on the other hand, Clay supported Adams because he felt that his supporters' interests would be best advanced by Adams rather than Jackson, or because Adams had promised to advance the interests of Clay's following, there would be nothing unsavory about any such bargain. Bargaining per se is not illegitimate or undesirable. On the contrary, it is central to the democratic process and can enhance the implementation of preferences.

A critical characteristic of any bargaining between direct election and a run-off is that it is worth no more than the ability of the candidates to deliver their following. Any bargain that depends on the shift of millions of voters has to be communicated publicly (although, of course, it may have both public and private components). Many of the voters will evaluate the alternatives differently than the candidate seeking to shift his following, and many of them will not follow.[22] In general, one would expect that any secret bargains involving private gain would be much easier to consummate in the Electoral College or a congressional contingency election than in a run-off involving millions of voters.[23]

Of course, unless the change to a run-off itself changed the distribution of votes, no run-off would have occurred in any election but that of 1860— as long as 40 percent of the votes would have been sufficient to elect or if the electoral vote system had been retained for the main election. But the possibility of a run-off might encourage minor parties and therefore reduce victory margins.

It is certainly true that two elections cost more than one and that some voters might lose interest, but this may be a reasonable price for the assurance of a popularly determined result. The risks of intrigue and violence and interference with an orderly transition seem not to be obviously greater with a run-off than with present contingency procedures.

V/Reflecting Popular Preferences

Neither the Electoral College nor direct election can always assure that popular preferences are accurately reflected in the final vote count. The faithless elector is a liability unique to the Electoral College, but it is less clear which system is superior in assuring a clear, honest, and accurate count of popular votes.

Faithless Electors

The problem of the faithless elector infuriates opponents of the Electoral College. Although, in practice, a trivial issue, it could seriously subvert the electoral process. The office of elector is an anachronism. The framers of the Constitution created it because they expected the Electoral College to have to choose among many state-based candidacies and because they did not anticipate a national party system that would narrow the number of candidates.

Electors almost immediately lost their function as independent decision-makers, and today, everyone expects them to vote as the plurality of voters in their state voted. An occasional elector, however, does violate that expectation and remind us that the integrity of the electoral process depends in part on the good faith of those chosen.

The first time an elector voted for someone other than the candidate in whose name he ran was in 1796, when an elector chosen as a Federalist voted for Thomas Jefferson.[1] The most recent was in 1976, when a Washington state Republican voted for Ronald Reagan. In the 180 years between those two elections, less than a dozen electors have miscast their votes, although six of them have done so since 1948.[2]

Less than a dozen faithless electors out of more than 17,000 do not constitute a serious problem, but on occasion, the possibilities have been troublesome. For example, the 1876 election was decided by a single electoral vote, and any one of the 185 Republican electors could have swung the election to Samuel Tilden. Ironically, although this action would have violated the spirit of the Electoral College, it would have brought the election into line with majority preferences.

A more serious problem is the possibility of systematic efforts to mobilize electors pledged to major candidates in order to bargain with the candidates for the support they have already earned or to force the election into the House of Representatives. For example, in 1960, Henry Irwin, an Oklahoma Republican elector, sent telegrams to all Republican electors asking if they would support a Byrd-Goldwater ticket. He hoped that enough southern Democrats would be willing to join Republican electors in support of such a ticket to win an Electoral College majority, thus denying the presidency to the "labor Socialist nominee." Ultimately, however, only Irwin cast votes for Byrd and Goldwater.[3] A number of comparable efforts were discussed in 1968.[4]

The faithless elector problem is unique to the Electoral College system. Although the faithless electors portray themselves as defenders of the fundamental values of the Republic, defenders of the Electoral College consider such electors a liability. Actually, the defenders' main argument against a constitutional amendment to eliminate the electors and automatically translate popular votes into electoral votes is that they feel such a trivial change is not worth the trouble of a constitutional amendment.[5]

A Clear, Honest, and Accurate Vote Count

Any election system, no matter how perfectly conceived, is a problem if it generates indeterminate results. At some point, the need for continuity in government demands that a decision be made. The office must be filled, and prolonged uncertainty and deadlock are liabilities in any system.

No electoral institution can guarantee that the "right" candidate wins. Direct election is the system most likely to assure that the candidate with the most support wins, but its superiority to the Electoral College is relative rather than absolute. If a candidate has an overwhelming superiority in popular support, he will win under any of the proposed arrangements. However, if an election is close, the situation becomes more difficult. Direct election is surely superior to its alternatives in measuring popular support, but by doing so in close elections, it simply mirrors a popular result that may, for practical purposes, be close to a tie. Since direct election cannot measure intensities of preference or preference orderings, the counting of first choice votes is itself slightly arbitrary (although certainly very reasonable). If a direct election is indeterminate (reflecting a virtual tie), its virtues are not very useful. In elections as close as those between Kennedy and Nixon (.2 percent) or between James A. Garfield and Winfield S. Hancock (.1 percent in 1880), any decision is slightly arbitrary. There is much to be said for a clear decision.

Defenders of the Electoral College have emphasized that the system has worked well in such cases. In 1880, Garfield led Hancock by less than ten thousand votes among nine million; yet the Electoral College translated those figures into a clear victory for Garfield, 214 to 155. We will never know whether John Kennedy actually had more first choice support among the voters than Richard Nixon in 1960, but his margin in the Electoral College was a healthy 303 to 219.

The great virtue of the Electoral College in most elections that have close popular votes is that it produces a clear-cut winner. Under the rules of the Constitution, these elections were not even close, and they produced victors most people seem to have thought should have won by other standards as well.

With the exception of the ill-fated 1876 election, which made a marginal electoral vote winner out of a clear popular vote loser, all Electoral College results are more one-sided than the popular vote results on which they are built.[6] The tradeoff is fairly clear. Although it may occasionally choose the wrong candidate,[7] the Electoral College normally exaggerates popular margins so that there is almost always a clear-cut victor by constitutional standards. As its defenders point out, the elections in which the Electoral College does not choose the candidate with the most votes are elections that, except for 1876, were virtual toss-ups anyway. If one is willing to accept the risk of choosing the candidate who came in a close second in popular votes, the Electoral College has the effect of a dignified, authoritative coin flip, biased in the direction of the popular leader. For the benefit of almost invariably exaggerating the victory margin in order to provide a decisive result, the Electoral College has the drawback of occasionally exaggerating the vote of the second place candidate into victory.

This way of resolving a virtual tie is reasonable if two conditions are accepted. The first is that elections won by as much as 52 percent of the two-party vote must be considered a toss-up. (Charles W. Bischoff has calculated that in two of the twelve elections between 1920 and 1964, the Democrats would not have won a majority of electoral votes until they had won more than 52 percent of the popular vote. He calculates that the Republicans would not have won two of those elections until they had won more than 51 percent of the popular vote.[8])

The second condition is that the Electoral College must be considered an acceptable tie-breaking mechanism, even though as such it discriminates against candidates who build up large concentrations of votes in some states, while losing others by small margins. Until the end of the era of the Solid South in the 1940s, this feature resulted in discrimination against the Democrats, but the two parties are now sufficiently competitive in all sections that the Electoral College no longer has a clearly partisan bias.

One reason why these issues about the clarity of the results are especially important is that fraud is not unknown in the United States. The honesty of the vote count affects the clarity of the choice of the president. As Theodore H. White notes:

> Those who report elections know, alas, that the mores and morality of vote-counting vary from state to state. The votes of Minnesota, California, Wisconsin and half a dozen other states are as honorably collected and counted as votes anywhere in the world. There are other states in the Union

where votes are bought, paid for and, in all too many cases, counted, manipulated and miscounted by thieves. The voting results of the valley counties of Texas are a scandal; so, too, are the voting results in scores of precincts of Illinois' Cook County; so too, in ward after ward of West Virginia, in the hills of Tennessee and Kentucky, and in dozens of other pockets of rural or urban machine-controlled slums.[9]

Proponents of both direct election and the Electoral College claim that their system is less vulnerable to fraud than the alternative, and each has a point.

Under the Electoral College system the payoffs of engaging in fraud vary from place to place. Precisely because it exaggerates small margins of popular votes, the Electoral College offers extraordinary leverage, and perhaps incentive, to those who would commit electoral fraud. Critics of the Electoral College emphasize that only a few thousand votes would have to be miscounted in a few states to reverse an election.

Defenders of the Electoral College observe that the situation can work the other way. Since the incentives for fraud are localized, it is much easier to deter. Since states that are won by large margins, as many are, do not present opportunity for fraud, fraud is a danger in few places, and in those, the authorities and likely victims can concentrate their efforts on deterrence with maximum efficiency. Only a prospective loser in a given state has an incentive for fraud, and that incentive exists only so far as there is a possibility of crossing the line between victory and defeat.

Under direct election, however, every stolen vote would count because all votes are counted equally. Deterrence would have to be effective wherever there was a danger of fraud, which could be almost anywhere. Some opponents of direct election imagine that a prospectively close race could result in an orgy of miscounting that would severely reduce the integrity of our elections, and three of the last five elections have been very close.

Of course, even under close elections, the amount of fraud necessary would be difficult to manage, especially if the other side was working just as hard. If only a single percentage point separated two candidates who shared 70 million voters, 700,000 votes would have to be added to the loser's total to reverse the outcome. A tenth of a percent difference would still leave 70,000 votes to make up.[10] Establishing national administration of presidential elections could minimize the possibilities of fraud, but some feel that that is too small a benefit to compensate for the loss of local control, and others fear that central administration would increase the possibilities for manipulation.[11]

Richard G. Smolka, a seasoned observer of U.S. elections, has suggested that the threat of electoral fraud is greatest when those who commit it—presumably, local officials—can directly benefit; thus local elections may be more vulnerable to fraud than others. If he is correct, then there is minimal danger of fraud in presidential elections under any vote-counting system, and dishonesty is not a problem that sharply distinguishes the alternatives.

Alleged fraud or extremely close elections can result in the demand for recounts. Since popular votes are generally closer than electoral votes, the demands may prove reasonable more often under direct election. Furthermore, since direct election proposals normally provide for run-offs as well as a main election, there could be two recounts: one to determine the necessity of a run-off and another to resolve the run-off. The result would be intolerable delays in identifying the winner.

The 1974 Senate election in New Hampshire illustrates some undesirable possibilities with close elections under direct voting. In that election, Republican Congressman Louis C. Wyman led Democrat John A. Durkin by 355 votes. For various reasons, some 15 percent of the votes were questioned. On a recount, Durkin won a ten vote victory, which was officially certified on November 27. Wyman appealed to the state's ballot law commission, which awarded the office to him by two votes, 110,926 to 110,924, on December 24. This result was, in turn, certified, superseding the previous result.

Since under Article I, section five of the Constitution, "each house shall be the judge of the elections, returns and qualifications of its own members," the Senate sent the problem to the Rules Committee, which, after reexamining the disputed ballots and deliberating, found itself unable to reach a conclusion. The Rules Committee put the issue before the entire Senate. Senate Republicans, fearing a partisan decision by the Democrat-controlled body, proposed a new election. With the help of some southern Democrats, they prevented the issues from coming to a vote. The deadlock continued until July 28, when Durkin agreed to a new election. The election, held September 16, was won by Durkin by a 54-to-43 margin. Senator Durkin was sworn in September 18, almost nine months after his colleagues had been seated.[12]

The New Hampshire situation was unusual for a sub-presidential election, and may be even more unusual for presidential elections. Even so, the risks involved in delays in filling the office of president are much greater than those posed by a vacant Senate seat. An unresolved presidential election is a possibility that should be avoided even at high cost; the liabilities and drawbacks of the Electoral College may be a reasonable price to pay.

On the other hand, a major source of the difficulties in the Durkin-Wyman recount was the use of paper ballots, which are still used in almost 20 percent of the nation's precincts (with the remainder using voting machines or punch card ballots).[23] Replacement of paper ballots with mechanical or electronic voting devices that automatically register votes might obviate both the possibility and the necessity for recounts and insure a more accurate count.

VI/The Nature
of the Party System

Changing the electoral system can be expected to change more than the ways in which votes are counted. It may have some effect on the distribution of votes itself. Candidates would alter their strategies, and even the number and identity of candidates might be changed. Similarly, the importance and vitality of various other electoral institutions, such as state political parties, might be affected.

The Two-Party System

In assessing the effect of the electoral system on the party system, two issues are often confused: first, whether or not a two-party system is desirable, and second, the effects of different electoral systems on the number of parties. Proponents of various plans tend not to dispute the desirability of the two-party system, but neither do they analyze in depth the reasons for its desirability. Judith Best cites "almost universal agreement" on the benefits of the two-party system and quotes a textbook on parties as saying that "[m]ore than any other American Institution, [the Electoral College system] consciously, actively and directly nourishes consensus."[1] Sayre and Parris emphasize that two parties offer a single choice, a moderating atmosphere, and an efficient basis for administering the government.[2] Longley and Braun, who support direct election, also count maintaining the two-party system among their criteria for evaluation of reforms but recognize "the legitimate right of potential third and fourth parties to electoral influence. . . ."[3] Many opponents of direct election want to discourage minor parties and often acknowledge no such right.

Presumably, there are tradeoffs in the choice of party systems. Clear and meaningful choices may come at the expense of consensus and moderation. A two-party system is desirable in part because it simplifies the choices into two alternatives, one of which will receive a clear majority and thereby a clear claim to office. In addition, having two parties is considered desirable by some because narrowing the options to two may tend to produce ambiguous and unclear alternatives, which make for moderated conflict. People are less likely to become intensely committed regarding vague and ambiguous alternatives than regarding clear and distinct ones. Losers are less likely to be bitter when the winner is not very much different from the loser.

However, such ambiguity and moderation may interfere with public choice and popular control. To some thinkers, democracy is to be found whenever there is competition for office, regardless of the nature of the choices.[4] Frequent complaints by others of "there's not a dime's worth of difference" suggest that a simple duality of moderate alternatives is not always fully satisfactory.

Multiparty systems can offer much more distinct and "meaningful" choices than two-party systems, but elections in multiparty systems are much less likely to yield a majority, or even a clear winner. Typically, there must be a second stage, such as coalition building in a parliamentary system or perhaps a run-off election where chief executives are directly elected. According to some who see a moderating influence in the two-party system, clear, meaningful choices might also become polarized alternatives wherein the losers are bitter and loath to accept election results.

Thus, there are reasons to criticize the two-party system, but these issues are not what divides proponents of different electoral systems. These proponents do, however, confront each other on the issue of which electoral arrangement is most likely to maintain a two-party system.

Both sides are partially correct in claiming that their alternative reinforces the two-party system and that the other one undermines it. To understand the dispute, we must distinguish between the number of parties and the closeness of competition between them.

The Electoral College does not encourage competition between the existing two parties in one-party areas because there is nothing to be gained for the weaker party until it can actually defeat the opposition in a given state. In the era of the Solid South, Republicans had little reason to make much effort in that region unless they would be able to concentrate their votes enough actually to win a state and receive all of its electoral votes. Similarly, Democrats have no reason to commit heavy resources to overwhelmingly Republican areas, since there would be no pay-off short of victory there.

Under direct election, no votes are wasted because of where they are cast. Every vote counts equally, no matter how strong the local opposition is. Direct election would therefore encourage vote-maximizing candidates and parties to seek support in every section of the country, thus encouraging state-level two-party competition in a way that the present system does not.

However, if what is meant by the two-party system is not the extent of competition throughout the nation, but rather the number of parties competing, the effects of the electoral alternatives are different. In this sense, the Electoral College discourages one kind of minor party and encourages another, while direct election treats all minor parties equally.

The Electoral College rewards regionally concentrated third parties and punishes national ones. This effect is vividly illustrated by the 1948 election, in which Dixiecrat Strom Thurmond and Progressive Henry Wallace each won 2.4 percent of the vote. Since the Dixiecrat votes were concentrated in several southern states, they were good for thirty-nine electoral votes. The comparable number of Progressive votes was dispersed throughout the nation, consequently yielding no electoral votes at all.[5]

Opponents of direct election contend that, by not discriminating against national third parties, that system actually encourages them. They argue that under a direct election system we would see more minor parties than we now do, at the net expense of the total vote for the two major parties and to the detriment of the prospect that the contest can be decided without a contingency election.

These arguments hinge on the alternative provisions for contingency election under direct voting. A simple plurality rule for direct election would not encourage any minor party that did not anticipate having more votes than anyone else and therefore winning the presidency. Alternatively, a rule that demanded that the winning candidate have 50 percent of the votes would enable a minor party with a tiny fraction of the votes to force a run-off if the major party votes were evenly divided.

Most proponents of direct election argue for a compromise contingency rule that falls between these two extremes: victory at 40 percent or more of the votes, and a run-off between the top two candidates below that. On the one hand, this contingency rule would assure that the winner did not have an embarrassingly small percentage of the votes and, on the other, it would demand that minor parties win a minimum of 20 percent of the vote before a run-off would be necessary. As we have seen, no major party candidate since Lincoln has received less than 40 percent of the votes, and Lincoln was less than a percentage point away. However, the opponents of direct election argue that minor party candidates would enter the contests in order to force a run-off, hoping for more leverage than their votes would otherwise merit.

Whether direct election with a run-off will encourage more minor parties to compete cannot be known until it is tried, but a recent study regarding primary elections is relevant. Bradley Canon has related factionalism in southern and border state Democratic primaries to the amount of competition from the Republican party and to the presence or absence of a provision for a run-off.[6]

Unlike previous researchers, Canon finds that the strength of the Republican party has little impact on the factional structure of Democratic gubernatorial primaries.[7] However, the possibility of a run-off has a striking effect: it reduces the proportion of votes going to the top candidate(s) and lowers the number of candidates receiving significant numbers of votes. Canon's analysis generates support for the idea that the existence of a run-off actively encourages more candidates to enter, thus reducing the proportion of the vote going to the top candidates.

This evidence suggests that a direct election system that provides for a run-off below 50 percent will probably encourage minor parties to enter more often than will a direct election that has no run-off at all. However, the differences may not be so striking on the national scene for two reasons. An individual candidate can get on the ballot in a southern Democratic primary more easily than a minor party can get on the national ballot, although the degree of difficulty depends on the nature of the election laws and is easily manipulated by them. Furthermore, the contrast between simple plurality and run-off below absolute majority is much greater than the contrast between the current Electoral College system and run-off below 40 percent. Nevertheless, Canon's analysis supports the contention that direct election with a run-off would encourage minor parties.

But even if a run-off encouraged minor parties from time to time, there is no reason to expect them to be continuing participants in the electoral process.[8] Since the presidency can be won only by a single candidate at a time, there is little direct potential payoff for any candidate who does not have a good prospect of winning the election. In this sense, the office of president itself is a major underpinning of the two-party system. French experience under the Fifth Republic also shows how an elective presidency has led to remarkable coalescence of a formerly fractionalized party system. Even with a run-off below 50 percent of the votes, French elections for both the presidency *and* the legislature have become largely contests between two coalitions.

In general, such manipulations of the electoral laws as the change to a direct election should not be expected to transform party systems by themselves. Douglas Rae, the leading student of the impact of electoral laws on party systems, puts it this way:

> It is clear enough that electoral systems exert genuine and systematic effects upon party competition. But . . . elections express the interplay of political forces which are enormously complicated and, of course, important. All manner of forces—social, economic, institutional, personal—express themselves in election results. Electoral laws only modify these outcomes in marginal degree.[9]

Federalism

Many defenders of the Electoral College have emphasized the reinforcement of federalism as a major advantage of the existing arrangements and argue that direct election would undermine the federal system. The major basis of federalism is the independent policymaking authority of the state governments, and the state-based election of congressmen and senators is a federal element in the national government itself. These would remain under direct election.

The main impact of direct election on federalism would presumably be limited largely to the role of the states in defining election laws and to the role of state parties in the presidential selection process. Some observers also anticipate that presidential candidates would pay less attention than they do now to state and local concerns if states were no longer the basic unit for counting votes, but this effect is less obvious.

Currently, the states have extensive authority in directing the administration of elections. The main limits on state authority in this area are nationally determined standards for voter eligibility, as defined by the Fifteenth, Nineteenth, Twenty-fourth, and Twenty-sixth Amendments to the Constitution.[10] Each state decides how parties and candidates qualify for a position on the ballot and how the ballot is to be arranged and establishes rules for registration, hours of voting, tally, and recount of votes.[11]

The vitality of the federal system may not be contingent on state control of issues such as these, but direct election would surely demand consideration of national policy regarding them. This necessity places a burden of clarification and specification on advocates of direct election. The most troublesome of these issues is access to the ballot. Richard Smolka summarizes:

> Who is entitled to be listed [on the ballot]? Who determines the nominee of a political party and how is that nomination decided? Can independent candidates without any party affiliation qualify for the ballot? May a candidate who has been denied the nomination of his party obtain a ballot listing as a new party or as an independent candidate?[12]

If all votes are to be counted equally in a single national total, all ballots ought to present exactly the same options. To assure that they did so, Congress would have to establish rules that would determine, for example, which of the thirteen candidates who qualified for the ballot for president in six or more states in 1976 would be on the national ballot.

A party's access to the ballot could be determined by percentages achieved in previous elections, but Congress or the courts might have to resolve disputes about which factional leader was a party's official nominee. For example, in 1976, Michigan courts had to decide which of two American Independent party factions deserved that party's label. Such a problem also can occur in a major party, as it did in 1860, when Stephen Douglas and John Breckenridge represented irreconcilable factions within the Democratic party. There would also have to be a national policy regarding the access of independent candidates, such as Eugene McCarthy, to a national ballot. Presumably, signatures would be collected, and standards set, either high or low, for the number of signatures necessary for a place on the ballot.

Under direct election, state boundaries would become irrelevant in counting votes, and the position of state parties in national campaigns might therefore be weakened. State political parties, once the most vital element of the national structure of party organization, have already seen their position eroded by the reform of the presidential nominating process and by the changing nature of political campaigns; direct election might continue that erosion.

VII/The Nature of the Choice

A decision about which system of electing the president is preferable depends on values, on priorities among those values, and on estimates of the consequences of change. No authoritative statement can be made here about a hierarchy of values or about the consequences of election systems that have not been tried. We can, however, suggest the implications of different values.

For example, if voter equality is an overriding issue, the Electoral College or any other system retaining electoral votes is seriously flawed. Only direct election assures that all votes will be counted equally, no matter where or by whom they are cast.

If having the candidate with the most votes win is the prime concern, the Electoral College is fatally flawed by the possibility that the runner-up in popular votes can win in electoral votes. But direct election does not guarantee that the candidate with the most support wins if there are more than two candidates. It does guarantee that the candidate with the most votes cannot lose any given election. But since direct election measures only first choice preferences, it cannot directly reflect intensities of preference or of distaste and therefore cannot assure that the candidate with the most votes is "most preferred."

The run-off between the top two candidates is designed to deal with the possibility that a candidate with a mere plurality of support will not be able to win unless he prevails over opponents who have an opportunity to unite against him. But even a run-off does not offer a foolproof method of assuring that the most preferred candidate is included. Under certain conditions with multiple candidacies, there is no way to identify the candidate with the most support, and consequently no way to guarantee his election. Direct election is superior to the Electoral College in assuring that the candidate with the most votes wins, but as a means of assuring that the candidate with the most support and the least opposition wins, its superiority to the Electoral College is relative rather than absolute.

The one point on which the case for direct election seems to be weakest and the case for the Electoral College seems to be the strongest is in yielding a clear result. All systems faithfully reflect overwhelming majorities of popular support, and when there are such clear majorities, it scarcely matters what kind of an electoral system is used. As election results become narrower, however, the Electoral College becomes more and more fallible in reflecting the relative strengths of the leading candidates. The direct election system is more precise. But a precise reflection of an election that is nearly a dead heat may not be very useful. When an election is close, what is needed may not be so much a precise reflection of deadlock as a clear result. At the cost of risking the choice of a runner-up, the Electoral College generally produces more decisive results than direct election would.

On the basis of the analysis in this essay, it is possible to arrive at a reasonable decision in support of direct election or of the Electoral College, depending on how one ranks the goals of accurately reflecting popular first choice preferences and of achieving a decisive result. The discussion about election systems is colored by the fact that the status quo is the Electoral College, which, in spite of risks and close calls has not produced a major malfunction for almost 100 years. This record produces a sense of security for its defenders. Any change involves uncertainty about prospective consequences, and proponents of direct election are placed on the defensive by predictions of dire consequences the possibility of which cannot be totally ignored. The Electoral College itself may seem just as likely to lead to dire consequences, but its defenders are able to point to years of relatively smooth operation and say that the potential disasters are highly unlikely and in practice have not been a problem. Thus, some of the structure of the argument is defined by what happens to be the status quo and what is not.

In one of the few analyses of the Electoral College debate that is not designed to make a case for one side or the other, Max Power observes that the different sides tend to argue from different premises, values, and modes of thinking and, therefore, to talk past each other. Proponents of direct election seem to use rational-deductive logic, and defenders of the Electoral College seem to use empirical-pragmatic reasoning.[1]

Neither kind of argument is flawless in its own terms, and each side tends to shift at some point to the grounds of the other. Proponents of direct election shift their grounds to pragmatic reasoning in defending a 40 percent threshold below which there would be a run-off between the top two candidates. Proponents of the Electoral College seem to acknowledge the one-person one-vote majority rule standard when they argue that the current system regularly produces a winner who meets that standard. These supporters of the Electoral College usually argue that the fact that a candidate might win without having the most votes is an anomaly rather than a virtue. In part, both these stances are dictated by circumstances, by the fact that one system is a known quantity and the other has not been tried.

If a new system of electing presidents were being designed today, it would surely be more like the direct election system than like the Electoral College, whose form was defined by eighteenth-century political realities.

Of course, we do not start from scratch, but with an electoral system that is over 150 years old and has adapted to drastically changing conditions. Thus, while no one would create this Electoral College *de novo* today, it is defended with a vigor that derives from decades of results that are considered satisfactory.

Notes

Chapter I

1.   Quoted in Neal R. Peirce, *The People's President: The Electoral College in American History and the Direct Vote Alternative* (New York: Simon and Schuster, 1968), p. 52.

2.   Lucius Wilmerding, Jr., argues that the framers did not mean to exclude the people from participating in the choice of the president or to have electors choose according to their own will without guidance by the people. They meant the Electoral College to be "a medium for ascertaining public will." See Lucius Wilmerding, Jr., *The Electoral College* (New Brunswick: Rutgers University Press, 1958), pp. 19–22.

3.   Peirce, op. cit., pp. 74–78, 309–311. See also Wilmerding, op. cit., Chapter Three.

4.   Wallace S. Sayre and Judith H. Parris, *Voting for President: The Electoral College and the American Political System* (Washington, D.C.: The Brookings Institution, 1970), p. 42. See also Peirce, op. cit., p. 119.

5.   In five Gallup polls between 1966 and 1977 (four of which were taken between 1966 and 1968), support for "a constitutional amendment eliminating the electoral college and basing the Presidential election on total popular vote throughout the country" ranged between 58 and 81 percent, while the opposition ranged between 12 and 22 percent.

In seven polls between 1948 and 1961 asking a slightly different question, an average of 56.4 percent favored change and 23.4 favored retention of the Electoral College. The percentage who understood the approximate meaning of the term "Electoral College" ranged between 32 and 42 percent.

6.   For a discussion of recent efforts to secure congressional approval for direct election, see Lawrence D. Longley and Alan G. Braun, *The Politics of Electoral College Reform,* 2nd ed. (New Haven: Yale University Press, 1975), Chapter 1. For a more comprehensive view, see Peirce, op. cit., Chapter 6: "Reform Efforts of Two Centuries."

7.   While James Madison of slaveholding Virginia was willing to yield the political weight of slaves in order to achieve direct election, many other southerners were not. See Peirce, op. cit., pp. 41–42.

8.   For a recent discussion, see Michael Margolis, "From Confusion to Confusion: Issues and the American Voter (1956–1972)," *American Political Science Review* 70 (March 1977), pp. 31–43.

9.   Some plans provide for electoral units other than congressional districts, but the number in each state would remain the same.

10.   Some plans would allocate votes according to the number of representatives alone, eliminating the two voters per state to reflect its representation in the Senate.

Chapter II

1.   See John H. Yunker and Lawrence D. Longley, "The Biases of the Electoral College: Who is Really Advantaged?" in Donald R. Matthews, ed., *Perspectives on Presidential Selection* (Washington, D.C.: The Brookings Institution, 1973), pp. 173–174; and Longley and Braun, op. cit., pp. 95–96.

2.   Yunker and Longley find that the correlation (Pearsonian r's) between state size and competitiveness was 0.09 in 1948, 0.33 in 1952, 0.18 in 1956, 0.25 in 1960, −0.02 in 1964, and 0.33 in 1968. Thus, all but 1964 confirm the hypothesis that large states tend to be more competitive most of the time. However, only two correlations were significant at the 0.05 level, and none at the 0.01 level. See Yunker and Longley, op. cit., pp. 199–200.

J. Harry Wray has computed for this project average winning percentages in presidential elections by five classes of state size between 1936 and 1976 (excluding 1968). The averages are, in descending order of state size, 56.7%, 60.1%, 61.4%, 60.4%, and 59.5%. Omitting the southern states, which tend to fall in the middle three categories, might make the relationship more linear, but in any case, the relationship between size and competitiveness is not strong, even if it is somewhat in line with the conventional wisdom.

3.   John F. Banzhaf III, "One Man, 3.312 Votes: A Mathematical Analysis of the Electoral College," *Villanova Law Review* 13 (Winter 1968), pp. 304–332.

4.   Ibid., p. 329.

5.   John H. Yunker and Lawrence D. Longley, "The Electoral College: Its Biases Newly Measured for the 1960s and 1970s," *Sage Professional Papers in American Politics,* Series 04-031, 3 (1976), pp. 1–25. Yunker and Longley report six different sets of figures for the Electoral College in the 1960s and 1970s, according to variations in population distribution and in theoretical assumptions. The results all follow the same basic pattern.

6.   Ibid., p. 14.

7.   Ibid., p. 12. A citizen-voter is considered by Banzhaf and by Yunker and Longley to be the number of citizens in each state, thus preserving relative sizes of states without taking into account differences in voting age populations and turnout. Yunker and Longley also make estimates based on turnout.

8.   Banzhaf, op. cit., p. 307.

9.   Ibid., p. 308.

10.   Ibid.

11.   Seymour Spilerman and David Dickens, "Who Will Gain and Who Will Lose Influence under Different Electoral Rules?" *American Journal of Sociology* 80 (September 1974), pp. 443–477.

12.   Ibid., pp. 452–453. Their unit of analysis is 416 congressional districts, excluding several at-large districts.

13.   See Yunker and Longley, "The Biases of the Electoral College," pp. 195–198; and Yunker and Longley, "The Electoral College," pp. 41–44.

14.   See footnote 2.

15.   Peirce, op. cit., p. 159; see also p. 261.

16.   Of course, since both the Senate and, to a degree, the Electoral College advantage small states, these two institutions do not have fully counterbalancing effects.

17.   *Wesberry v. Sanders,* 376 U.S. 1 (1964).

18.   Alexander M. Bickel, *Reform and Continuity: The Electoral College, the Convention and the Party System* (New York: Harper and Row, 1968), p. 10.

19.   Sayre and Parris, op. cit., pp. 136–137; see also pp. 46–47.

20.   Yunker and Longley, "The Biases of the Electoral College," pp. 190–195.

21.   However, their finding that suburban residents are advantaged is at odds with the generalization that deprived groups are the beneficiaries.

22.   Before southern blacks could vote in large numbers, they were especially disadvantaged in the Electoral College by the fact that their main political enemies, southern whites, were advantaged in the Electoral College by controlling the electoral votes of the southern black *and* white populations. Under direct voting schemes, these southern whites would have had only the weight of their own votes.

23.   Spilerman and Dickens, op. cit., pp. 460–473. See also Melvin J. Hinich and Peter C. Ordeshook, "The Electoral College: A Spatial Analysis," *Political Methodology* 1 (Summer 1974), pp. 1–29 (especially p. 15); Hinich and Ordeshook, in a theoretically rich analysis, find a bias *against* blacks in the Electoral College but observe that it has attenuated over time.

24.   They use ecological regression for their estimates. This technique depends on assumptions that may not be met in their data. Douglas Blair has done an analysis that uses survey data over five elections to estimate the voting behavior of demographic groups, rather than ecological regressions of a single election. Blair's findings are much more congruent with those of Yunker and Longley; see Douglas Blair, "Electoral College Reform and the Distribution of Voting Power," U.S. Senate, *Judiciary Committee, Hearings on the Electoral College and Direct Election,* February 1977, pp. 503–514.

25.   Banzhaf, op. cit., pp. 323–324.

26.   But see Steven J. Brams and Morton D. Davis, "The 3/2's Rule in Presidential Campaigning," *American Political Science Review* 68 (March 1974), pp. 113–134; and Hinich and Ordeshook, op. cit., pp. 5–7.

27.   Longley and Braun, op. cit., pp. 82–83.

28.   Quoted in Matthews, ed., op. cit., p. 218.

29.   Ibid., p. 203.

Chapter III

1.   For further background, see Peirce, op. cit., pp. 82–86.

2.   Ibid., pp. 92–93, offers further detail.

3.   A lengthier treatment can be found in ibid., pp. 86–92.

4.   Judith V. Best, *The Case Against Direct Election of the President: A Defense of the Electoral College* (Ithaca: Cornell University Press, 1975), p. 53.

5.   Ibid., pp. 52–53, citing the study by Paul Leland Haworth, *The Hayes-Tilden Disputed Presidential Election of 1876* (Cleveland: The Burrows Brothers Co., 1906).

6.   For further detail, see Peirce, op. cit., pp. 100–109; and Longley and Braun, op. cit., pp. 1–7.

7.   Peirce, op. cit., p. 105.

8.   In Mississippi, Kennedy received less than half of the combined total vote for Democratic and unpledged electors. He would have had to do considerably better in Alabama to retain his national vote lead.

9.   Best, op. cit., Chapter 2, *passim.*

10.   Peirce, op. cit., pp. 317–321. Peirce is aware that "In each case, however, a vote shift larger over-all than the mathematical minimum first indicated would undoubtedly have been necessary, since any significant change in voting patterns would have been general, not selective in a few crucial states" (p. 317). See also Svend Petersen, *A Statistical History of the American Presidential Elections* (New York: Ungar, 1963), for figures on minimum vote shifts necessary to change all but the most one-sided election outcomes.

11.   Peirce, op. cit., p. 321.

12.   Longley and Braun, op. cit., p. 11.

13.   Best, op. cit., p. 74. Peirce is aware of this problem; see footnote 9, *supra*.

14.   Sayre and Parris, op. cit., p. 136.

15.   Best, op. cit., pp. 65; 70; 79–80.

16.   Arguments like these will be considered more extensively in Chapter VII.

17.   It is possible to allow voters to rank their preferences and to add votes in such a way as to reflect second and third choices, etc. The main problem with this system is that it lends itself to "strategic voting," wherein voters may misrepresent their preferences in order to enhance the prospects of their first choice. For example, a voter may rank his second choice last to reduce the chances that his second choice will defeat his first. See Richard A. Musgrave and Peggy B. Musgrave, *Public Finance in Theory and Practice,* 2nd ed. (New York: McGraw-Hill, 1976), pp. 103–111, for a discussion of these issues.

18.   The definitive mathematical treatment of this issue is Kenneth J. Arrow, *Social Choice and Individual Values,* 2nd ed. (New York: John Wiley & Sons, 1963). The Musgraves, loc. cit., make the issue understandable to the general reader. See Max S. Power, "Logic and Legitimacy: On Understanding the Electoral College Controversy," in Matthews, ed., op. cit., pp. 204–237, for a good discussion in the context of the Electoral College. Steven J. Brams and Peter C. Fishburn have proposed a scheme called "approval voting" to deal with this problem. Under this system, a voter can vote for as many candidates as he chooses in a given contest but cannot vote more than once for any candidate. The candidate with the most votes wins. See "Approval Voting," their paper prepared for delivery at the 1977 Annual Meeting of the American Political Science Association, Washington, D. C. (forthcoming in April).

19.   Daniel A. Mazmanian, *Third Parties in Presidential Elections* (Washington, D.C.: The Brooking Institution, 1974), pp. 69–77, considers specific cases in presidential elections across two centuries.

20.   In Virginia, the only southern state in which Lincoln was on the ballot, he received 1.1 percent of the votes. (South Carolina was still choosing electors in the legislature.)

21.   See Peirce, op. cit., pp. 358–359; and Nelson Polsby and Aaron Wildavsky, *Presidential Elections,* 4th ed. (New York: Charles Scribner's Sons, 1976), p. 253.

Chapter IV

1.   We must, of course, consider the possibility that the basic election procedure affects the likelihood that a contingency election will be desirable or necessary. Defenders of the Electoral College argue that that system discourages minor parties and therefore, by itself, reduces the prospects that such parties will emerge and drive down the vote percentages of leading candidates. The argument is that by discouraging the proliferation of options, the Electoral College enhances the likelihood that most of the votes will be distributed between only two candidates, thus minimizing any need for a contingency election. This argument deserves careful consideration, which it will receive in Chapter V.

2.   Peirce, op. cit., pp. 47–49.

3.   Ibid., pp. 133–134. If no vice-presidential candidate receives a majority of vice-presidential electoral votes, the contingent election takes place in the Senate. Such an election has taken place only once, in 1837. Martin Van Buren won a majority of electoral votes for president, but his running-mate, Richard M. Johnson, was boycotted by Virginia's electors. The Senate elected Johnson by a vote of 33 to 16.

4.   Ibid., pp. 65–71. The framers had not anticipated this possibility because they had

not anticipated parties. This problem was corrected by the Twelfth Amendment, which provided for separate ballots for president and vice-president and under which Jefferson would have won the original count of electoral votes.

5. Ibid.

6. See Best, op. cit., p. 89.

7. *Congressional Quarterly Guide to Elections* (Washington, D.C.: Congressional Quarterly, Inc., 1967), pp. 206–208, 225; and Peirce, op. cit., pp. 82–86.

8. Sayers and Parris, op. cit., p. 65.

9. Best, op. cit., pp. 87–88.

10. Ibid., p. 87.

11. Ibid.

12. Ibid., pp. 88, 83.

13. Ibid., pp. 88–89. (Reprinted from Judith Best: *The Case Against Direct Election of the President.* Copyright © 1971 by Judith Vairo Best, copyright © 1975 by Cornell University Press. Used by permission of Cornell University Press.)

14. The 1976 election was in a sense a closer call than 1968, because a shift in fewer votes could have changed the outcome. But such a shift in 1976 would have produced a runner-up president, rather than a contingency election, as in 1968.

15. Best, op. cit., pp. 98–99.

16. James A. Michener, *Presidential Lottery: The Reckless Gamble in Our Electoral System* (New York: Random House, 1969).

17. Ibid., p. 13.

18. For example, see ibid., pp. 13–25, 91–95.

19. Longley and Braun, op. cit., pp. 7–17.

20. Best, op. cit., pp. 104–105.

21. Sayre and Parris, op. cit., pp. 74–76.

22. See Harvey Zeidenstein, *Direct Election of the President* (Lexington, Mass.: Lexington Books, 1973), Chapter 5.

23. In the literature on French presidential elections under the Fifth Republic, there is no evidence of any kind of bargaining, unsavory or otherwise, between the main election and the run-offs. See Elijah Ben-Zion Kaminsky, "The Selection of French Presidents," in Matthews, ed., op. cit., for an excellent discussion of the subject.

Chapter V

1. This act provoked a response that showed that even then electors were expected to reflect the preferences of the people who chose them. A Federalist complained, "What, do I chuse Samuel Miles to determine for me whether John Adams or Thomas Jefferson shall be President? No! I chuse him to *act,* not to *think*." Quoted in Peirce, op. cit., p. 64.

2. Ibid., pp. 121–126; and Best, op. cit., Chapter 5.

3. Peirce, op. cit., p. 107.

4. Michener, op. cit. See Peirce, op. cit., pp. 126–127, for a discussion of the unpledged elector movements in the post-World War II South, wherein elector candidates run unpledged or conditionally pledged, seeking to bargain with leading candidates or to force the election into the House.

5. Sayre and Parris, op. cit., pp. 100–101.

6. See Peirce, op. cit., pp. 315–316.

7.   As we have seen, the candidate with the most votes lost in 1876, 1888, and perhaps in 1960.

8.   Peirce, op. cit., pp. 141–145. Bischoff performed these calculations by adding uniform percentage shifts to the votes of each party. He then determined the point for each election and each party that would have produced a bare Electoral College majority, given the distribution of votes among states in that election.

9.   Quoted in Best, op. cit., p. 203. See also Peirce, op. cit., pp. 236–239.

10.   Peirce, op. cit., pp. 285–289. Peirce argues that the prospects of an outcome that is too close to determine a winner are "miniscule." He quotes Tom Wicker to the effect that our closest election (between Garfield and Hancock in 1880, won by 9,457) would proportionately be the equivalent of a 69,000 vote plurality in 1964 and even larger pluralities as the size of the electorate grows. "Admittedly," Peirce argues, "this is a narrow margin on a national basis. But it would still be a clear and unambiguous national plurality, barring allegations of voting irregularity on a scale that the country has in fact not experienced in modern times." He contends that it is statistically doubtful that there would be more than one election in a century with a popular vote so close that there would be legitimate dispute about the result. He does acknowledge that "[i]t is in this area of the speed in the count and challenge procedure, rather than in obtaining, finally, a conclusive national count, that the direct vote for president raises the most serious problems."

11.   Best, op. cit., p. 209.

12.   *Congressional Quarterly Almanac* 31 (1976), pp. 699–702, 928.

13.   Richard G. Smolka, "Possible Consequences of Direct Election of the President," *State Government* 50, 3 (Summer 1977), p. 139.

Chapter VI

1.   Best, op. cit., pp. 105, 212. The textbook quoted is Austin Ranney and Wilmoore Kendall, *Democracy and the American Party System* (New York: Harcourt, Brace and World, 1956), p. 508.

2.   Sayre and Parris, op. cit., p. 4.

3.   Longley and Braun, op. cit., p. 75.

4.   Joseph A. Schumpeter, *Capitalism, Socialism and Democracy* (New York: Harper and Row, 1942), is identified with this view.

5.   For a careful and illuminating analysis of the effects of alternative systems on third parties, see Melvin J. Hinich, Richard Mickelson, and Peter C. Ordeshook, "The Electoral College Versus a Direct Vote: Policy Bias, Reversals, and Indeterminate Outcomes," *Journal of Mathematical Sociology,* 4 (1975), pp. 3–35, but especially pp. 12–24.

6.   Bradley Canon, "Factionalism in the South: A Test of Theory and a Revisitation of V. O. Key," *American Journal of Political Science,* forthcoming.

7.   The leading source is V. O. Key, Jr., *Southern Politics in State and Nation* (New York: Alfred A. Knopf, 1949).

8.   See Mazmanian, op. cit., pp. 68–69.

9.   Douglas Rae, *The Political Consequences of Electoral Laws* (New Haven: Yale University Press, 1967), pp. 83–84. See also Zeidenstein, op. cit., Chapter 5; and Max S. Power, "A Theoretical Analysis of the Electoral College System and Proposed Reforms," Ph.D. dissertation, Yale University, 1971, pp. 205–219.

10.   See Chapter 1, p. 23.

11.   See Smolka, op. cit.

12.   Ibid., p. 134.

Chapter VII

1.   Max S. Power, "Logic and Legitimacy: On Understanding the Electoral College Controversy," in Matthews, ed., op. cit., pp. 235–237.

Selected Bibliography

Selected Bibliography

Banzhaf, John F., III. "One Man, 3.312 Votes: A Mathematical Analysis of the Electoral College." *Villanova Law Review* 13 (Winter 1968), pp. 304–322.

Best, Judith. *The Case Against Direct Election of the President: A Defense of the Electoral College.* Ithaca: Cornell University Press, 1975.

Bickel, Alexander M. *Reform and Continuity: The Electoral College, the Convention and the Party System.* New York: Harper and Row, 1968.

Blair, Douglas. "Electoral College Reform and the Distribution of Voting Power." U.S. Senate, Committee on the Judiciary, *Hearings on the Electoral College and Direct Election,* 95th Congress, 1st Session. Washington, D.C.: U.S. Government Printing Office, 1977, pp. 503–514.

Brams, Steven J., and Morton D. Davis. "The 3/2's Rule in Presidential Campaigning." *American Political Science Review* 68 (March 1974), pp. 113–134.

——, and Peter C. Fishburn. "Approval Voting." *American Political Science Review* (forthcoming).

Congressional Quarterly Guide to Elections. Washington, D.C.: Congressional Quarterly, Inc., 1976.

Diamond, Martin. *The Electoral College and the American Idea of Democracy.* Washington, D.C.: American Enterprise Institute, 1977.

Hinich, Melvin J., Richard Mickelson, and Peter C. Ordeshook. "The Electoral College vs. a Direct Vote: Policy Bias, Reversals and Indeterminate Outcomes." *Journal of Mathematical Sociology* 4 (1975), pp. 3–35.

——, and Peter C. Ordeshook. "The Electoral College: A Spatial Analysis." *Political Methodology* 1 (Summer 1974), pp. 1–29.

Longley, Lawrence D., and Alan G. Braun. *The Politics of Electoral College Reform.* 2nd ed. New Haven: Yale University Press, 1975.

Mazmanian, Daniel A. *Third Parties in Presidential Elections.* Washington, D.C.: The Brookings Institution, 1974.

Michener, James A. *Presidential Lottery: The Reckless Gamble in Our Electoral System.* New York: Random House, 1969.

Petersen, Svend. *A Statistical History of the American Presidential Elections.* New York: Frederick Ungar, 1963.

Peirce, Neal R. *The People's President: The Electoral College in American History and the Direct Vote Alternative.* New York: Simon and Schuster, 1968.

Polsby, Nelson, and Aaron Wildavsky. *Presidential Elections.* 4th ed. New York: Charles Scribner's Sons, 1976.

Power, Max S. "A Theoretical Analysis of the Electoral College System and Proposed Reforms." Ph.D. dissertation, Yale University, 1971.

——. "Logic and Legitimacy: On Understanding the Electoral College Controversy." *Perspectives on Presidential Selection.* Ed. Donald R. Matthews. Washington, D.C.: The Brookings Institution, 1973.

Rae, Douglas W. *The Political Consequences of Electoral Laws.* New Haven: Yale University Press, 1967.

Sayre, Wallace S., and Judith H. Parris. *Voting for President: The Electoral College and the American Political System.* Washington, D.C.: The Brookings Institution, 1970.

Smolka, Richard G. "Possible Consequences of Direct Election of the President." *State Government* 50, No. 3 (Summer 1977), pp. 134–140.

Spilerman, Seymour, and David Dickens. "Who Will Gain and Who Will Lose Influence under Different Electoral Rules?" *American Journal of Sociology* 80 (September 1974), pp. 443–477.

U.S. Senate. Committee on the Judiciary. *Hearings on the Electoral College and Direct Election.* 95th Congress, 1st Session. Washington, D.C.: U.S. Government Printing Office, 1977.

Wilmerding, Lucius, Jr. *The Electoral College.* New Brunswick: Rutgers University Press, 1958.

Yunker, John H., and Lawrence D. Longley. "The Biases of the Electoral College: Who Is Really Advantaged?" *Perspectives on Presidential Selection.* Ed. Donald R. Matthews. Washington, D.C.: The Brookings Institution, 1973.

——. "The Electoral College: Its Biases Newly Measured for the 1960s and 1970s." *Sage Professional Papers in American Politics.* Series 04-031, 3 (1976), pp. 1–25.

Zeidenstein, Harvey. *Direct Election of the President.* Lexington, Mass.: Lexington Books, 1973.